# THE
# ULTIMATE
# BOOK OF
# CONFIDENCE
## FOR
## *Teen Girls*

# OTHER BOOKS BY

## *M.J. Fievre*

### FOR YOUNG ADULTS

*Badass Black Girl*

*Female, Gifted & Black*

*The Book of Awesome Black Women*

*Black and Resilient*

*Walk Boldly*

*Resilient Black Girl*

*Radiant Faith*

*Black Brave Beautiful*

*Empowered Black Girl*

## FOR KIDS

*Young Trailblazers: The Book of Black Inventors and Scientists*

*Young Trailblazers: The Book of Black Heroes and Groundbreakers*

*Haiti A to Z*

*A Cat Named Sam*

*The Ocean Lives There*

## FOR ADULTS

*Happy, Okay?*

*Your Work from Home Life*

*Raising Confident Black Kids*

# THE ULTIMATE BOOK OF CONFIDENCE FOR

## *Teen Girls*

### A SURVIVAL GUIDE FOR NAVIGATING LIFE WITH EASE

## M.J. FIEVRE

CORAL GABLES

Cover & Layout Design: Megan Werner
Cover Illustration: Briddy / stock.adobe.com

For permission requests, please contact the publisher at:
Mango Publishing Group
2850 S Douglas Road, 2nd Floor
Coral Gables, FL 33134 USA
info@mango.bz

For special orders, quantity sales, course adoptions and corporate
sales, please email the publisher at sales@mango.bz. For trade
and wholesale sales, please contact Ingram Publisher Services at
customer.service@ingramcontent.com or +1.800.509.4887.

The Ultimate Book of Confidence for Teen Girls: A Survival Guide
for Navigating Life with Ease

Library of Congress Cataloging-in-Publication number:
2023938982
ISBN: (pb) 978-1-68481-419-0 (hc) 978-1-68481-420-6
(e) 978-1-68481-421-3
BISAC category code YAN051200, YOUNG ADULT NONFICTION /
Social Topics / Self-Esteem & Self-Reliance

Printed in the United States of America

# TABLE OF CONTENTS

# TABLE OF CONTENTS

# INTRODUCTION

## Unveil Your Power

Welcome to *The Ultimate Book of Confidence for Teen Girls*—a dedicated guide filled with inspiring stories, practical advice, and empowering resources tailored to help navigate through the labyrinth that adolescence can be. This book is your handy guide to embracing the best version of yourself while transitioning into adulthood, a phase often brimming with excitement, change, uncertainty, and wonder.

As a teenager, you are at a pivotal moment in life's grand journey. You are discovering who you are, your preferences, your passions, and your place in the world. The teenage years serve as the scaffolding for your future self. It's a time filled with self-exploration, personal growth, understanding, and the inevitable grappling with self-doubt and introspection. This is where *The Ultimate Book of Confidence for Teen Girls* steps in, offering you a supportive roadmap as you embark on your unique journey.

This book is more than a guide; it's your companion, encouraging you to embrace your individuality while learning how to tackle the challenges that come your way. It's designed to bolster your confidence, resilience, and self-esteem, providing the essential tools to navigate your formative teenage years. Our journey through these pages will empower you to acknowledge your strengths, overcome hurdles, and unlock your potential to lead a fulfilling and successful life.

This comprehensive and meticulously curated guide explores a broad spectrum of topics. These are all instrumental in shaping your confidence, building a strong sense of self-worth, and facilitating personal growth. As we delve deeper, you'll uncover the secrets to:

*   Building a robust foundation of self-esteem and self-confidence that empowers you to believe in your inherent abilities and potential.

*   Developing a positive body image that helps you appreciate your unique beauty and navigate societal pressures tied to appearance and body standards.

*   Fostering and nurturing healthy relationships with friends, family, and potential romantic partners, focusing on the importance of effective communication, setting boundaries, and mutual support.

*   Learning how to tackle challenges and adversity head-on, demonstrating resilience, and understanding the importance of bouncing back from setbacks stronger than before.

*   Managing stress and mental health effectively, with an emphasis on prioritizing your well-being and equipping yourself with coping strategies to weather the stormy periods of adolescence.

* Setting personal, academic, and career goals while understanding the power of perseverance, effective time management, and the power of motivation in achieving these goals.

* Exploring your interests and passions, understanding the role of hobbies, and engaging in extracurricular activities in fostering a well-rounded sense of self.

* Preparing for the future by making informed decisions about your education, career, and life planning, and embracing the limitless opportunities that lie ahead.

* Lastly, embracing your unique journey, reflecting on your personal growth, and appreciating the importance of remaining authentic to your values.

Throughout the book, we'll share inspiring real-life stories from individuals who have faced challenges head-on and emerged victorious. These stories will remind you that you are not alone and can overcome any obstacle that stands in your way.

Additionally, this guide includes interactive elements to encourage engagement with the content. Writing prompts, reflection questions, and hands-on activities are designed to help you apply what you've learned, fostering a deeper understanding of your goals and dreams.

*The Ultimate Book of Confidence for Teen Girls* is not just a book; it's a journey toward self-discovery, growth, and empowerment. As you turn each page, you'll uncover your inner strengths, embrace your unique qualities, and grow your confidence to strive into a life you design for yourself.

So here we are, ready to embark on this exciting, transformative journey together. Brace yourself to uncover your inner power, embrace your authentic self, and unleash the confidence within you waiting to be unlocked. The aim is to help you survive the world and conquer it while staying true to yourself.

This book will open doors to the many aspects of your life and self that you may not have considered before. Each chapter will help you understand a new dimension of your being, presenting you with the tools to mold each facet into a shape that best represents who you are and aspire to be. Whether you need guidance on tackling a problem, encouragement to stand up for yourself, or a reminder of your worth, this book is here.

In these pages, you'll find many inspirational quotes and powerful messages from globally recognized figures, authors, and even fictional characters. These will remind you of your strength and potential and motivate you to persist, even when the going gets tough.

Moreover, you will learn from stories of individuals who have not just walked the path you are about to embark on but have left a mark for others to follow. Through their unique journeys, these role models demonstrate the resilience, tenacity, and strength required to turn dreams into reality.

It is vital to understand that your journey will be unique to you. Each challenge, each victory, each setback, and each triumphant moment is yours and yours alone. This book reminds you that no matter the path you tread, you have the power to shape your future and influence your destiny.

*The Ultimate Book of Confidence for Teen Girls* does not seek a one-size-fits-all solution; instead, it offers guidance that you can tailor to your unique experiences. It provides a framework you can adapt and build upon, helping you become the best version of yourself.

In essence, this book is about believing in yourself and your potential. It's about knowing your worth and never settling for less. It's about embracing the journey of self-discovery and growing into a confident, resilient, and empowered individual.

So, let's take the first step together. The time has come to invest in yourself, your dreams, and your future. The time has come for you to begin the journey with *The Ultimate Book of Confidence for Teen Girls*. Here's to the exciting, challenging, inspiring journey that awaits you!

# CHAPTER 1

## Embrace Your Authentic Self

You've just embarked on an important journey that leads not merely through the pages of a book but into the depths of your self-understanding and potential. It's a journey that will challenge, uplift, and ultimately empower you to embrace the confidence that already resides within you.

The path you've stepped onto is exciting, with you at the helm steering your course. It's not just any journey; it's your voyage into a world filled with self-discovery, courage, and strength. This book—*The Ultimate Confidence Guide for Teenage Girls*—is designed with you in mind, an intimate exploration of your unique spirit, power, and potential.

As you turn the page to the first chapter, you will be greeted with the concept of authenticity, the cornerstone of self-confidence. You might wonder, "Why authenticity? What makes it so crucial?" Authenticity is more than just being yourself; it's about understanding and accepting your individuality and expressing it without fear or reservation. It is this genuine self-expression that forms the crux of self-confidence.

Self-acceptance and self-awareness are the twin pillars upon which your journey to self-confidence will be built, each playing a vital role. Self-acceptance involves embracing all facets of yourself, your strengths, and your weaknesses without judgment. Conversely, self-awareness invites you to understand your emotions, motivations, and actions more deeply. Together, they fortify your confidence, giving you the resilience and poise to face life's challenges head-on.

During this initial phase of your journey, we will delve into subjects that may seem unfamiliar yet are essential to your growth. We'll explore what authenticity truly means, how personal values shape your identity, and how recognizing your strengths can empower you to handle life's difficulties with grace and conviction.

But rest assured, this isn't a solo expedition. You're not navigating these sometimes-uncharted waters alone. You'll be guided by the wisdom and experiences of remarkable women who've walked this path before, like Malala Yousafzai and Emma Watson. Through their stories of courage, resilience, and authenticity, these individuals will serve as your compass, your guiding light as you traverse the landscape of self-confidence.

So, as you step into this fascinating realm of self-discovery, get ready to unlock your potential and ignite the spark of authenticity that lies within you. You're about to embark on a transformative journey that promises to instill a more profound sense of self-confidence and empower you to be your most authentic self. Brace yourself; it's time to set sail on this extraordinary voyage of self-exploration and self-belief. Welcome to the journey of a lifetime—the journey to a more confident, more empowered you.

# REAL-LIFE STORIES

## *Malala Yousafzai*

## A FEARLESS CRUSADER
## FOR GIRLS' EDUCATION

Imagine facing adversity, daring to raise your voice for what you believe in, despite knowing it could cost you dearly. This is the story of Malala Yousafzai, a young woman whose fierce authenticity and unshakeable commitment to her cause echo across the globe, inspiring millions.

Born in the Swat Valley of Pakistan, Malala was just a young girl when she was at the epicenter of a cultural and political storm. She was a mere fifteen years old when she dared to speak out against the Taliban's oppressive regime, advocating the right of girls to receive an education, and her defiance made her a target. In a horrifying act of violence meant to silence her, a Taliban gunman shot Malala.

Yet, it was this brutal act that, paradoxically, amplified her voice rather than quietening it. Malala's spirit proved unbreakable. The attack didn't make her recoil in fear; instead, it fanned the flames of her resolve. She became a beacon of hope and resilience, turning her trauma into a catalyst for change on a global scale. Her story is a testament to the extraordinary power of embracing one's authentic self and standing unwaveringly by one's beliefs.

Undeterred by the challenges and threats she faced, Malala continued to fight for girls' education. Her passion and perseverance resulted in her advocacy resonating far beyond her hometown. It echoed across borders, spotlighting the plight of millions of girls denied their fundamental right to education.

The world took notice. In 2014, at seventeen, Malala became the youngest-ever recipient of the Nobel Peace Prize. Her achievement was a testament to her courageous advocacy and a powerful validation of her authenticity and belief in her cause.

Today, Malala stands as the epitome of resilience and determination, a young woman who stood unflinchingly in the face of terror for a cause she believed in. Her story inspires us to embrace our authentic selves, voice our truths fearlessly, and never underestimate an individual's power to effect change. Malala's story serves as a beacon, illuminating the path toward authenticity, courage, and self-confidence. Her spirit and resolve remind us that, even against the odds, our authentic selves hold the power to forge extraordinary paths and inspire change on a global scale.

## Emma Watson
### ADVOCATING FOR EQUALITY AND HARNESSING THE POWER OF AUTHENTICITY

Equally inspiring in her pursuit of authenticity is Emma Watson, a familiar face to many as Hermione Granger in the "Harry Potter" series. However, beyond her notable role in this beloved franchise, Emma has harnessed her authenticity and platform to effect change, particularly in gender equality.

Born and raised in Paris and Oxfordshire, Emma was just a child when she catapulted to stardom. Amid the whirlwind of fame, she never lost sight of her passion for education and fairness, a testament to her authentic self. After completing her degree in English literature from Brown University, Emma embraced a new role beyond the silver screen and truly embodied her core values and beliefs.

In 2014, Emma was appointed as a UN Women Goodwill Ambassador. She launched the "HeForShe" campaign from this esteemed platform to invite men and boys to join the fight against the negative stereotypes and discrimination women and girls worldwide face. Her speech at the United Nations General Assembly meeting was a defining moment in her advocacy work, boldly tackling issues of gender inequality and calling for systemic change.

Emma's advocacy for gender equality isn't a performance—it embodies her genuine commitment to fairness and her belief in the potential for change. Her journey emphasizes that staying true to your authentic self involves recognizing your passions and leveraging your strengths to make a positive impact. By embracing her role as an advocate, Emma has inspired millions to join the conversation about gender equality, illuminating the path toward a more equal world.

Emma Watson's story illustrates the profound impact individuals can have when they are true to themselves and their values. Her authenticity and her passion for social justice have made her a force to be reckoned with, not just in the film industry but also in gender advocacy. Emma's journey underscores the importance of embracing our authentic selves, remaining true to our values, and using our strengths to contribute positively to the world.

# *Zuriel Oduwole*

## ADVOCATE FOR GIRLS' EDUCATION
## AND FILMMAKER

Zuriel Oduwole is a vivid example of a young person embracing her authentic self, utilizing her voice and passion for advocating for causes dear to her. Born in Los Angeles, California, Zuriel's heritage blends Nigerian and Mauritian roots, providing her with a rich multicultural perspective that underpins her work and advocacy.

From a young age, Zuriel demonstrated an undeniable knack for storytelling, a trait she harnessed to spark change. At just nine years old, she began making short films as part of a school project, not knowing that this foray into filmmaking would eventually lead her onto an international platform.

Zuriel's films often spotlight educational inequities facing girls in Africa, a cause she champions with unwavering dedication. Her commitment is far from superficial—she uses her platform to raise awareness about the importance of educating girls. She has leveraged her filmmaking skills to amplify this critical issue on a global scale.

In addition to her filmmaking, Zuriel became the youngest person to be profiled by Forbes at just ten years old. This recognition was a testament to her commitment to her cause and the authenticity with which she pursued it. Zuriel's poise and dedication have earned her invitations to meet with prominent world leaders—including presidents and prime ministers—underscoring her significant impact even at a young age.

By sixteen, Zuriel had already interviewed thirty-one heads of state, spoken in twenty-one countries on girls' education, and was listed in *New African* magazine's list of "100 Most Influential People in Africa." These accolades speak volumes about her authenticity, determination, and commitment to making a difference.

Zuriel's story is a beacon for young girls worldwide, illuminating the incredible possibilities that lie ahead when one embraces their authenticity. Her journey is a testament to the profound impact one can have when one harnesses their unique abilities and remains true to their values. Through her films and advocacy, Zuriel encourages us all to believe in the power of our voices and the importance of staying true to our authentic selves.

## *Yara Shahidi*
## AUTHENTICITY EMBODIED
## IN ART AND ACTIVISM

Yara Shahidi's story is one of embracing authenticity, intertwining passions for acting and activism, and fearlessly standing for what she believes in. This young actor, born in Minneapolis, Minnesota, has carved her path to influence, cementing her place as a powerful voice of her generation.

Yara has significantly impacted Hollywood with her natural talent and charisma. She first came into the limelight as the savvy, outspoken Zoey Johnson in the TV show *Black-ish*. Her performance was so compelling that she got her spin-off series, *Grown-ish*, where her character navigates the complexities and challenges of young adulthood. These roles have made Yara a household name, but they've also served as a platform for communicating issues close to her heart.

But Yara's influence extends beyond the TV screen. An ardent advocate for diversity and inclusion, she uses her platform to elevate underrepresented voices, exemplifying the power of authenticity in sparking meaningful conversations. She cofounded Yara's Club, a digital platform partnered with the Young Women's Leadership Network that provides an online mentorship program to end poverty through education.

She's also an active participant in political discourse, using her fame to encourage her peers to become more politically active. In 2018, she started "Eighteen x 18," a creative platform to engage her generation in politics. The initiative successfully boosted youth voter turnout, demonstrating Yara's influence and authenticity.

Yara Shahidi's story is a testament to the power of authenticity. By embracing her true self, she has become a beacon for many young girls globally, demonstrating that success comes from staying true to your values and using your platform to effect change. Yara's journey is a shining example of the power of authenticity, proving that embracing our unique selves can inspire others and create meaningful change in the world.

These young women represent the power and potential of embracing authenticity, showcasing the impact teenagers can make when they align their passions and values with their actions. Their stories remind us that age does not limit one's ability to inspire change and make a difference.

# PRACTICAL ADVICE AND TIPS

## Reflect on Personal Values

At the essence of who we are, our values serve as the fundamental principles guiding our lives. They are the threads weaving the intricate tapestry of our character. As such, they carry profound significance, and a deeper exploration into these guiding principles is a worthwhile endeavor. It's not simply about recognizing what you stand for or fervently believe in; it's about understanding why these values are vital to you.

Reflecting on your values helps illuminate the path you wish to tread, especially during challenging times when uncertainties may cloud your judgment. It is helpful to journal your thoughts as you reflect. It could be a list or a free-form mind map—whatever suits your style. Be open and honest with yourself in this process. Doing so sets a sturdy foundation, a reliable compass that aligns with your most authentic self.

## Discover and Celebrate Your Strengths

We are all bundles of unique strengths, abilities, and talents, some of which we might not even know. The next crucial step is giving yourself the space and time to identify these strengths. Start with a blank sheet and jot down all your strengths—intellectual, emotional, creative, physical. Don't rush this process; let it flow naturally. You might be surprised by the number of strengths you identify, many of which you might have overlooked.

Each strength you possess, no matter how grand or subtle, is vital in shaping your confidence and self-acceptance. Celebrate these strengths and give yourself credit for them. It's not boasting; it's acknowledging your potential and empowering yourself to use these strengths as stepping stones toward a more confident, more authentic you.

## Choose Positive Role Models

The influence of role models in our lives is often understated. These torchbearers inspire us, demonstrating the qualities we desire to emulate. They reflect the possible, extending our horizons and enriching our personal growth.

As you choose your role models, select those who resonate with your values and mirror the attributes you aspire to develop. You may find them in various walks of life—from celebrated figures like Malala Yousafzai and Emma Watson to everyday heroes in our communities or even within your family circle. Learn from their experiences, triumphs, and resilience in the face of challenges. Let their journeys fuel your determination to stay authentic.

## Practice Self-Compassion

One of the most critical elements in this journey toward self-acceptance is the practice of self-compassion. It is a gentle reminder to treat yourself with kindness, the same kindness you would generously extend to a close friend. It recognizes that, like every other person, you will make mistakes, you will stumble, and you will have flaws. But these are not shortcomings or failings; these are part and parcel of the human experience.

It's essential to understand that your perceived flaws do not diminish your value, worth, or deservingness of love and acceptance. Remember to speak kindly to yourself, especially during times of difficulty or disappointment. When you practice self-compassion, you're nurturing your self-acceptance, fortifying your resilience, and empowering yourself to bounce back stronger from life's adversities.

# WRITING PROMPTS AND REFLECTION QUESTIONS

* What does being authentic mean to you? Consider how embracing authenticity could fuel your self-confidence and self-acceptance. Reflect on this in your journal or a personal diary.

* Recall a situation where you faced a difficult decision. How did your values influence your decision-making process? What did this experience teach you? Writing about this can provide valuable insights.

* Reflect on your strengths. How have these traits helped you navigate challenging situations or achieve your goals? How can you further develop these strengths?

# KEY TAKEAWAYS

**Embrace your authentic self by understanding and staying true to your values.**

*Authenticity* means being true to who you are. It involves knowing your values, beliefs, and desires and living a life that aligns with them. Embracing your authenticity means refusing to compromise your beliefs or values to fit in or please others. In practice, it might mean standing up for what you believe in, even when it's unpopular, or pursuing a path that feels right for you, even if it's not what others expect. Remember, there is only one you in the world, so value your uniqueness and let your true self shine.

**Recognize and celebrate your unique strengths and abilities.**

We all have strengths and talents, things we are naturally good at or skills we have honed over time. These include academic abilities, artistic talent, leadership skills, problem-solving capabilities, or empathy toward others. Recognizing your strengths and talents helps build confidence and provides a sense of self-worth. Appreciate your unique abilities and use them to pursue your passions and positively impact the world around you.

**Learn from inspiring role models.**

Role models play a crucial role in our personal development. They provide us with real-life examples of how to overcome challenges, achieve goals, and live life authentically. People like Malala Yousafzai and Yara Shahidi teach us through their lives about resilience, courage, and the power of standing up for what we believe in. Learn from their stories, perseverance, and victories. Let their journeys inspire you and guide you on your path.

**Practice self-compassion and self-acceptance to build confidence and resilience.**

Self-compassion involves being kind and understanding toward yourself. It's about accepting that you're human and, like everyone else, you have strengths and weaknesses. You will make mistakes, and that's okay. Instead of being harsh and critical toward yourself, show the same kindness and understanding that you would offer a friend. This mindset fosters resilience, enabling you to learn from your mistakes rather than being defeated by them. With self-compassion, you can build a strong foundation of self-confidence that can help you navigate life's challenges with grace and resilience.

# INTERACTIVE ACTIVITIES AND EXERCISES

* **Value Exploration:** Compile a list of your top ten personal values. Rank them in their importance to you and consider how they influence your decisions and actions. This will provide a snapshot of the principles that guide you.

* **Strengths Collage:** Here's an exciting project—create a collage showcasing your strengths. Use images, words, or phrases that symbolize your talents and abilities. This collage will be a visual reminder of your strengths, boosting confidence whenever needed.

# QUOTES TO INSPIRE AND MOTIVATE

"To be yourself in a world that is constantly trying to make you something else is the greatest accomplishment."

—RALPH WALDO EMERSON

"When we embrace who we are, the world embraces us back."

—OPRAH WINFREY

"You are imperfect, permanently and inevitably flawed. And you are beautiful."

—AMY BLOOM

"Never be bullied into silence. Never allow yourself to be made a victim. Accept no one's definition of your life; define yourself."

—HARVEY FIERSTEIN

# Focus on Role Models

**Malala Yousafzai:** Malala's story offers lessons in courage, resilience, and the power of staying true to one's values. Despite adversity, her unwavering commitment to her beliefs led to profound accomplishments and global impact.

**Emma Watson:** While Emma is known widely for her film roles, her true character shines through her passionate advocacy for gender equality. Her determination to use her platform to raise awareness about women's rights has had a global resonance. Her story is a testament to the impact one can make by remaining authentic and committed to their cause.

**Zuriel Oduwole:** Zuriel's story is an impressive tale of passion and dedication. At an incredibly young age, she embarked on a path of advocacy for girls' education in Africa and has since continued to elevate the issue globally. Despite her age, Zuriel has proven that staying true to oneself and one's cause can result in significant social change.

**Yara Shahidi:** Yara's journey as a celebrated actor and influential advocate underlines the power of authenticity. Her commitment to her roles, both on-screen and off, illustrates the potential impact of young voices in pressing societal issues. Embracing her true self, Yara has become a beacon of inspiration, showing that success stems from adhering to one's values and leveraging one's platform for positive change.

# EMBRACING THE DANCE

As a teenager, my social life revolved around a struggle to fit in. I was constantly trying to mold myself into someone I thought others would like, and often that meant hiding parts of my true self. I had always loved dancing. Something about moving to the rhythm of music filled me with pure joy. But there was a problem: I wasn't good at it. I was rather clumsy, and my attempts at dancing needed to be more graceful. Afraid of ridicule, I kept this passion a secret.

In my junior year of high school, a talent show was announced. Despite my fear, a part of me yearned to participate. The idea of dancing freely on stage was both terrifying and exciting. After weeks of internal debate, I mustered the courage to sign up.

With the talent show date looming, I spent countless hours after school practicing in my basement, tripping over my feet, and replaying dance tutorials. While I made little improvement, my sheer joy while dancing was undeniable.

On the day of the show, my stomach was a whirl of butterflies. As I waited for my turn backstage, the fear of embarrassment nearly overwhelmed me. But then, the music started, and I stepped onto the stage. My mind screamed at me that I was making a mistake, but I started dancing anyway.

Yes, I missed a few steps and was not the most skilled dancer on that stage. But as I moved to the music, something incredible happened. I began to let go of my fear, and instead, I embraced the joy of dancing. The more I danced, the more the audience responded to my energy and enthusiasm.

After the performance, I was met with applause and cheers. To my surprise, many peers approached me to share how much they loved my performance—not because it was perfect, but because it was genuine, passionate, and brave.

That experience taught me the importance of embracing my authentic self. I learned that perfection isn't always what people admire; instead, it's authenticity, courage, and passion. From then on, I promised myself never to hide my true interests and passions for fear of not being good enough. It's our quirks, our unique passions, and our authenticity that make us who we are. And that's worth celebrating.

# EMBRACING AUTHENTICITY

As we conclude this opening chapter, it's clear that the importance of embracing your authentic self can't be overstated. We've journeyed together through a terrain shaped by authenticity, personal values, and the power of inherent strengths. These are foundational pillars on the path to self-confidence, and we've only started exploring them.

Reflecting on the narratives of extraordinary individuals like Malala Yousafzai, Zuriel Oduwole, and Emma Watson, it's evident how each found strength in authenticity. Their experiences are diverse, yet they share a common thread—each embraced their unique path, standing tall in the face of adversity. Their stories serve as a beacon, illuminating the path we're on.

This journey toward greater self-confidence and self-acceptance is inherently personal and intimately yours. Each stride you take toward discovering, understanding, and embracing your unique qualities is a step toward becoming the empowered individual you envision. There's a potent alchemy in realizing that your authenticity is not merely a trait; it's a superpower.

You are a mosaic of unique qualities, strengths, and talents. Together, these form the essence of who you are, and the world needs this authentic you. The world awaits your unique voice, your particular talents, and your distinct perspective. Embrace them, nurture them, and let them shine.

So, here you stand at the end of the first chapter, better equipped to appreciate the power of authenticity. Remember to carry these insights as you prepare to turn the page and embark on the next chapter. After all, they are the first steps on your journey to a more fulfilling and authentic life.

# CHAPTER 2

# Build Confidence and Self-Esteem

Having laid a solid foundation of understanding your authentic self in our first chapter, we now venture into uncharted territories in Chapter 2 of *The Ultimate Book of Confidence for Teen Girls*. This new journey is replete with practical techniques and strategies crafted with a single goal in mind—fostering your confidence and self-esteem.

Our quest will navigate through critical areas, such as confidence-building exercises that you can integrate into your daily life. We will explore the power of positive self-talk, which helps build and maintain confidence over time. Alongside this, we will delve into the importance of self-compassion, a critical yet often overlooked element in cultivating self-esteem. Finally, we'll learn about setting boundaries, a skill that enables you to assert yourself while maintaining respectful relationships with others.

Guiding us through this exploration, we'll have the inspirational stories of role models who have braved this path. Celebrities like

Zendaya and Millie Bobby Brown have often publicly discussed their journeys with self-confidence and self-esteem. Their experiences and insights offer a real-world perspective on the strategies we'll explore in this chapter.

Embarking on this chapter is about more than gaining knowledge—it's about empowering yourself. It's about fostering your inner strength and resilience and embracing them fully. This chapter is a stepping stone on your path to becoming a confident, self-assured individual who can handle any challenges that come your way.

So, strap in for this exciting exploration of confidence-building strategies and techniques. It's time to discover and nurture your inner strength; there's no better moment than now. Let's dive into this invigorating chapter!

# REAL-LIFE STORIES

*Zendaya*

## DEFYING STEREOTYPES AND EMBRACING SELF-CONFIDENCE

Zendaya Coleman, known simply as Zendaya, stands out as a beacon of inspiration and a stellar example of defying stereotypes in the modern world. A multifaceted talent, she is an acclaimed actress, a sensational singer, a successful entrepreneur, and much more. Her journey, marked by remarkable milestones, teaches us that you can achieve anything when you believe in yourself and cultivate self-confidence.

From humble beginnings as a Disney Channel star, where she graced our screens in shows like *Shake It Up*, Zendaya has ventured far and wide, making an indelible mark in the entertainment industry. Her compelling performances in critically acclaimed productions, such as *Euphoria* and *The Greatest Showman*, have won her accolades and proved her mettle as a versatile artist. Yet, amid her success, she never lost sight of her influence on young minds.

Passionate about encouraging her fans, particularly young women, to embrace their authenticity, Zendaya regularly uses her platform to spread messages of self-confidence and self-esteem. She advocates the importance of being true to oneself and boldly challenging societal norms and expectations. From speaking about body image issues to discussing her experiences as a young woman of color in Hollywood, she addresses a range of critical issues with sensitivity and maturity.

Moreover, she hasn't stopped at words—she has taken concrete action. Her fashion line, Daya by Zendaya, promotes inclusivity and diversity, underscoring her belief that everyone deserves to feel beautiful and confident. Her story is a testament to the transformative power of self-confidence when it's deeply rooted in authenticity.

# Millie Bobby Brown

## RISING ABOVE CHALLENGES WITH CONFIDENCE AND POSITIVITY

Born in Spain and raised in England, Millie Bobby Brown shot to global fame for her role as the enigmatic Eleven in the hit Netflix series *Stranger Things*. Aged just twelve when she took on this iconic role, Millie was thrust into the public eye. However, despite the sudden fame and the inevitable challenges that came with it, Millie has displayed an extraordinary level of maturity and resilience.

Her young career has been a rollercoaster ride—filled with breathtaking highs and challenging lows. However, Millie's approach to these experiences offers precious lessons in handling success and adversity with grace, confidence, and positivity. Despite encountering cyberbullying and intense public scrutiny, she has maintained her poise and stayed true to her authentic self.

Indeed, Millie has gone a step further, transforming her challenges into a broader cause. She leverages her influential platform to promote kindness, positivity, and self-acceptance. As UNICEF's youngest-ever Goodwill Ambassador, Millie advocates for children's rights. She speaks out against bullying—issues she is acquainted with.

Like Zendaya, Millie is not just a role model in terms of her career achievements. Her attitude, her spirit, and her approach to life's challenges make her a source of inspiration for young women across the globe. Her story teaches us that with confidence, positivity, and a never-give-up attitude, you can rise above any challenge and turn adversities into opportunities for growth.

# *Chloe Kim*
## FEARLESS ATHLETE AND
## CONFIDENCE EMBODIED

Chloe Kim's story is a testament to the power of self-confidence and courage in pursuing personal goals, even in the face of immense pressure and competition. This globally recognized snowboarding prodigy was born to South Korean immigrant parents in Long Beach, California.

Chloe's journey in snowboarding began at the tender age of four, and her talent was evident from an early age. By the time she was thirteen, Chloe was already performing professionally. Still, she was too young to compete in the 2014 Sochi Winter Olympics.

When she turned seventeen, Chloe had a historic run at the 2018 Winter Olympics in Pyeongchang, South Korea, becoming the youngest woman to win an Olympic snowboarding medal. Her record-breaking performance showcased her remarkable ability to thrive under pressure, a testament to her unwavering confidence.

Off the slopes, Chloe's authenticity and self-assured demeanor continue to shine. She openly discusses the pressures and expectations she experiences and how she navigates them, helping to inspire a new generation of athletes to pursue their passions fearlessly.

Chloe's infectious personality and confidence have made her a positive role model for young people worldwide. She encourages others to embrace their individuality, demonstrating that confidence comes from within and is critical to overcoming adversity. Chloe Kim's story is a resounding reminder of the power of self-confidence and resilience in achieving extraordinary feats.

# Rishitha Senthilkumar
## EMBODYING CONFIDENCE THROUGH INNOVATION AND LEADERSHIP

Rishitha Senthilkumar's story is of youthful brilliance, unwavering confidence, and the desire to make a difference. This young inventor and innovator, born in Chennai, India, is making her mark in the STEM (Science, Technology, Engineering, and Mathematics) world.

From an early age, Rishitha showed a keen interest in science and technology. Her passion for learning and problem-solving quickly led her to the world of invention. She invented the "Portable Retinal Scanner," a device that has the potential to revolutionize the detection and prevention of diabetic retinopathy, a common diabetes complication leading to blindness.

Yet, Rishitha's contribution to the world continues beyond her inventions. Recognizing the need for accessible STEM education, she founded EduSTEM, an initiative providing comprehensive STEM resources for students and educators. EduSTEM's work is dedicated to making STEM fields accessible and inclusive for all, reflecting Rishitha's belief in equality and education.

Rishitha's incredible confidence in her abilities and willingness to take risks have been instrumental in her journey. Her dedication, innovation, and commitment to her values show that confidence and self-belief are critical to making a difference.

Through her inventions and leadership in EduSTEM, Rishitha Senthilkumar embodies the powerful impact of youthful confidence. Her story encourages young people worldwide to believe in their abilities, embrace their interests, and use their strengths to impact their communities positively.

# PRACTICAL ADVICE AND TIPS

## Practice Positive Self-Talk:
### THE LANGUAGE OF SELF-LOVE

In the quest for self-confidence, the words you utter to yourself matter enormously. They form the soundtrack of your life, influencing your moods, perceptions, and overall outlook. Harness the power of positive self-talk by transforming your internal dialogue—notice when negative thoughts creep in, interrupt them, and consciously replace them with positive affirmations. Regularly remind yourself of your strengths, achievements, and potential. Instead of focusing on flaws or failures, highlight your capabilities and growth. By doing so, you'll reinforce a healthy self-concept, bolster your self-esteem, and foster a sense of optimism.

## Set Boundaries:
### THE ART OF PROTECTING YOUR SPACE

One of the most empowering aspects of building self-confidence is learning to set healthy boundaries. These invisible lines serve as your defense mechanism, protecting your self-esteem and mental well-being from external negativity or over-demanding circumstances. It is preserving your energy for what truly matters to you.

Understand that saying no is okay when situations do not align with your values, needs, or capacity. This isn't about being selfish—it's about practicing self-care. As you respect your boundaries, you'll find that others will, too. Doing so will not only prevent burnout but also promote respect and improve your relationships in the long run.

## Celebrate Small Victories:
### THE JOY IN EACH STEP

On the path to self-confidence, every step counts—every achievement, no matter how minor it may seem, is worth recognition. Embrace the habit of celebrating your small victories. Did you speak up in a meeting today? That's courage. Did you finish a project? That's diligence. Each accomplishment, each positive action, is a testament to your abilities and progress.

Acknowledging these moments boosts your confidence and reinforces your self-belief. It helps you realize that success is not just about reaching a distant destination—it's also about appreciating the journey and the growth that comes with it.

## Embrace Self Compassion:
### THE KINDNESS WITHIN

Lastly, self-confidence and self-esteem flourish in the soil of self-compassion. Treat yourself with the same kindness, patience, and understanding you'd extend to a dear friend.

Remember, everyone—yes, everyone—has flaws and makes mistakes. It's part of being human.

Rather than berating yourself for your mistakes, view them as opportunities for learning and growth. Understand that your flaws don't devalue you—they make you unique. Accepting your imperfections doesn't mean resigning yourself to them. Instead, it allows you to acknowledge them and seek growth. By practicing self-compassion, you'll feel more confident and at peace with yourself.

# WRITING PROMPTS AND REFLECTION QUESTIONS

* Reflect on a time when you felt confident and self-assured. What factors contributed to those feelings? How can you recreate those conditions in your everyday life?

* How do you currently practice self-compassion? How can you improve your self-compassion to better support your self-esteem and confidence?

* Consider the role models discussed in this chapter. What aspects of their confidence and self-esteem do you admire? How can you apply their lessons to your life?

# KEY TAKEAWAYS

**Build confidence and self-esteem through positive self-talk, setting boundaries, and celebrating small victories.**

Building confidence and self-esteem is a crucial aspect of your growth journey. To build your confidence, incorporate positive self-talk into your daily routine. Challenge negative thoughts and replace them with positive affirmations. Additionally, learn to set personal boundaries that prioritize your needs and well-being. Say no when necessary and express your thoughts and feelings assertively. Lastly, remember to celebrate your small victories, no matter how insignificant they may seem. Every step forward, no matter how small, brings you closer to your goals and strengthens your belief in your abilities.

**Practice self-compassion to support your mental well-being and self-esteem.**

Practicing self-compassion is key to supporting your mental well-being and self-esteem. Being kind to yourself, especially during a struggle or failure, can profoundly affect your mental health. Self-compassion involves treating yourself with the same kindness, care, and understanding that you would extend to a friend in a similar situation. Remember, it's okay to make mistakes and experience setbacks. These are opportunities to learn and grow rather than indications of personal failure.

**Learn from inspiring role models like Zendaya and Millie Bobby Brown, who embody confidence and self-assurance in the face of challenges and successes.**

Role models can be a source of inspiration and greatly influence your journey toward building confidence. Consider the examples of successful young women like Zendaya and Millie Bobby Brown. These remarkable individuals embody confidence and self-assurance in their professional and personal lives. Despite their young age, they have navigated the challenges and successes in their careers with extraordinary grace and determination. Their stories can provide valuable lessons in resilience, self-belief, and maintaining authenticity in all endeavors.

# INTERACTIVE ACTIVITIES AND EXERCISES

* **Confidence-Boosting Visualization:** Find a quiet space and close your eyes. Visualize a moment when you felt confident and self-assured. Recall the details of that moment, including your thoughts, feelings, and surroundings. Practice this visualization technique regularly to help reinforce positive feelings of confidence and self-esteem.

* **Positive Affirmation Journal:** Create a journal dedicated to positive affirmations and self-praise. Write at least one positive affirmation or accomplishment that highlights your strengths and abilities daily. Review your journal regularly to remind yourself of your achievements and build self-esteem.

# QUOTES TO INSPIRE
# AND MOTIVATE

"Believe in yourself! Have faith in your abilities! Without a humble but reasonable confidence in your own powers, you cannot be successful or happy."

—NORMAN VINCENT PEALE

"You gain strength, courage, and confidence by every experience in which you really stop to look fear in the face. You are able to say to yourself, 'I lived through this horror. I can take the next thing that comes along.' "

—ELEANOR ROOSEVELT

"No one can make you feel inferior without your consent."

—ELEANOR ROOSEVELT

"To love oneself is the beginning of a life-long romance."

—OSCAR WILDE

# Focus on Role Models

**Zendaya:** Zendaya's confidence and self-esteem shine through her work as an actress, singer, and entrepreneur. Her determination to challenge stereotypes and societal norms is an inspiring example of how embracing our authentic selves can lead to success and empowerment.

**Millie Bobby Brown:** Millie's ability to rise above challenges with confidence and positivity demonstrates the power of self-belief and resilience. Her commitment to promoting kindness and using her platform for good reminds us of the impact we can have when we stand firm in our convictions and stay true to ourselves.

**Chloe Kim:** Known as one of the best snowboarders in the world, Chloe Kim has won numerous medals at the Winter X Games and the Winter Olympics. Chloe's confidence shines on and off the snowboarding slopes, and her ability to perform under pressure is awe-inspiring.

**Rishitha Senthilkumar:** Rishitha is a teenage inventor, innovator, and founder of EduSTEM. This initiative provides STEM resources for students and teachers. She's made a substantial impact in the STEM world with her inventions. She has displayed great confidence in pursuing her passion for science and technology.

# FINDING MY VOICE

There was a time when my confidence and self-esteem were at an all-time low. As a teenager, I was painfully shy and always afraid of saying the wrong thing. My fear of judgment kept me from expressing myself. I often found myself going along with the crowd, even if I disagreed with what they were doing.

One day, I decided to join the school's debate team on a whim. I remember standing in the hall, staring at the sign-up sheet, my heart pounding. Standing up in front of others and expressing my opinion was terrifying. Still, something inside me urged me to take the leap.

My first few debate club meetings were challenging. I stammered, I stuttered, I lost my train of thought. But with each passing week, I got better. The more I practiced, the more I found my voice. And, to my surprise, people listened. They respected my opinions and valued my insights. I realized that I had something meaningful to say and my voice mattered.

In my first real debate, I stood before the school and spoke passionately about environmental conservation. When I finished, I was met with applause, and I could feel a surge of pride coursing through me. I had done it! I had faced my fears, and I had succeeded.

From that moment on, my confidence grew. I wasn't afraid to voice my opinions, to stand up for what I believed in, or to step out of my comfort zone. Joining the debate team was one of the best decisions I ever made. It helped me build my confidence and self-esteem and taught me the importance of self-expression and the power of my voice. This experience laid the foundation for the woman I am today—confident, assured, and unafraid to be myself.

# HARNESSING THE POWER OF CONFIDENCE

As we close this transformative chapter, we've delved deep into a collection of practical strategies to build and sustain confidence and self-esteem. Each technique—positive self-talk, boundary-setting, celebrating small victories, or embracing self-compassion—is crucial in your self-confidence toolbox.

These techniques are more than merely theoretical. They're dynamic, action-oriented habits you can weave into your daily life. By consciously practicing positive self-talk, you alter your internal dialogue to a more empowering one. By setting boundaries, you defend your emotional space, permitting yourself to prioritize self-care. By celebrating small victories, you acknowledge your progress, fueling your self-belief. And through self-compassion, you create a nurturing inner environment that fosters resilience and self-acceptance.

Intertwined with these practical approaches, we've drawn inspiration from the stirring stories of remarkable individuals like Zendaya and Millie Bobby Brown. Their narratives demonstrate the immense power of confidence and self-assurance, illustrating how these qualities can be harnessed to navigate challenges, seize opportunities, and make a positive impact.

As we move forward, let these role models' stories serve as a beacon, guiding you toward heightened self-confidence and self-esteem. Their journey is a testament to the transformative power of self-belief, resilience, and authenticity.

Remember, the path to self-confidence is not a straight line. It's a personal journey filled with peaks and valleys, progress, and setbacks. But with each step you take, know that you are growing, learning, and becoming more attuned to your strengths. Hold firm to your convictions, embrace your inner strength, and continue to believe in your worth. You are capable and powerful and deserve the utmost confidence and self-esteem. Cultivating these traits is not a destination but a journey that shapes a stronger, more self-assured you.

# CHAPTER 3

# Navigate Peer Pressure and Social Challenges

This exciting chapter promises to equip you with an arsenal of strategies and insights to tackle and overcome common challenges every teenage girl encounters. We'll be delving deep into essential life themes such as handling peer pressure with grace, dealing effectively with various social challenges, and fostering a resilient spirit that is not easily discouraged.

Our expedition into these captivating topics will begin by focusing on the significant issue of peer pressure. We'll tackle this complex situation head-on, providing you with tools to navigate these pressures without compromising your true self. We'll then focus on dealing with social challenges, exploring how you can respond effectively, and ensuring these situations enhance rather than hinder your personal growth.

Next, we'll cultivate resilience, a critical trait that can guide you through the trials of life. Understanding and developing resilience can help you maintain a positive outlook, even when facing difficulties. This emotional strength will allow you to bounce back from setbacks and learn from experiences, strengthening your character and self-esteem.

Further enhancing our exploration of these fundamental topics, we'll spotlight conflict resolution and assertiveness. We'll unravel the mystery of how to manage conflicts effectively and tactfully, ensuring mutual respect and understanding. Additionally, we will focus on assertiveness, helping you confidently communicate your needs and wants while respecting others.

We'll look to real-life role models for inspiration and wisdom. We'll highlight the journey of renowned personalities such as Selena Gomez and young innovator Gitanjali Rao. By examining their life stories, we can draw inspiration and learn invaluable lessons that can be applied to our lives. These figures embody the qualities of courage, perseverance, and determination that we will delve into during our exploration of confidence-building.

As we venture through this chapter, get ready to acquire and refine the skills needed to navigate the complex landscape of social situations. These new tools will empower you to confidently, effectively, and positively engage with your world. This chapter will guide your journey as you develop the skills and attitudes needed to confidently face the world as a teen girl. Prepare yourself for a transformative journey as we dive into Chapter 3 of *The Ultimate Book of Confidence for Teen Girls*!

# REAL-LIFE STORIES

## *Selena Gomez*

## OVERCOMING SOCIAL CHALLENGES
## AND MENTAL HEALTH STRUGGLES

Selena Gomez, a globally recognized singer, actress, and producer, is an inspiring figure who has bravely battled social challenges and mental health struggles throughout her career. As a young woman who grew up in the limelight, Selena encountered many challenges, many of which were amplified by her public status. However, rather than succumbing to these pressures, she faced them head-on.

Her experiences with mental health have been a significant part of her journey. Despite the stigmatization often associated with these issues, Selena bravely shared her struggles with the world. Her decision to seek professional help and speak candidly about her battles with anxiety and depression has demonstrated her resilience and paved the way for open conversations about mental health.

By using her platform to shine a light on these topics, Selena has shown her determination to overcome personal obstacles while striving to lessen the societal stigma associated with mental health issues. Her journey is a testament to the power of resilience and provides hope to others facing similar challenges.

# Gitanjali Rao

## PURSUING PASSION DESPITE PEER PRESSURE AND SOCIAL CHALLENGES

Another exceptional role model is Gitanjali Rao, a young innovator named *TIME*'s first-ever Kid of the Year. Despite her age, Gitanjali has made remarkable strides in her scientific pursuits while navigating the complex landscape of peer pressure and the social challenges of being a teenager.

From a young age, Gitanjali showed a keen interest in science and innovation. Despite the pressures from her peers and the doubt cast by naysayers, she remained steadfastly committed to her passion. Her unique journey is characterized by her dedication to her interests and unwavering resolve to stay true to her goals, even in the face of adversity.

Her inspiring story showcases the remarkable feats one can achieve when they do not let external pressures deter them from their path. Gitanjali's grit and determination have made her a symbol of resilience for young people worldwide, encouraging them to pursue their passions relentlessly, despite the social challenges they may face.

# Marsai Martin

## PIONEERING YOUNG HOLLYWOOD WITH CONFIDENCE AND CREATIVITY

Marsai Martin's story is a testament to the power of confidence, creativity, and the courage to challenge the status quo. This dynamic young actress and producer, born in Plano, Texas, is carving out her unique space in Hollywood.

Best known for her role as Diane Johnson on the critically acclaimed television show *Black-ish*, Marsai displayed her acting chops at a young age. With her quick wit and natural talent, she quickly became one of the most memorable characters on the show, resonating with audiences nationwide.

However, Marsai's ambitions continued beyond acting. At just fourteen years old, she became the youngest executive producer in Hollywood history with her film *Little*, a comedy in which she also starred. In navigating the competitive world of Hollywood, Marsai has shown maturity and confidence far beyond her years, successfully juggling the roles of actress and producer.

Marsai's accomplishments highlight her commitment to breaking barriers and creating opportunities for representation. Her production company, Genius Productions, is dedicated to producing content that showcases diverse stories, embodying her belief in inclusivity and equal representation.

Marsai Martin's journey is an inspiring example of how self-belief and perseverance can help you break barriers and achieve great things. She has turned the pressures of Hollywood into a platform for expressing her creativity and promoting representation, setting a powerful example for young people everywhere.

# Nandi Bushell
## BEATING THE DRUMS WITH CONFIDENCE AND PASSION

The story of Nandi Bushell, a young drummer from Ipswich, England, is a thrilling tale of passion, confidence, and unyielding determination. Despite her young age, she is a force to be reckoned with in music, standing as a testament to the power of self-belief.

At the tender age of five, Nandi began playing the drums, quickly revealing an extraordinary talent for her age. She quickly gained recognition by covering popular songs from various rock bands, which she posted on her YouTube channel. Her drumming skills, which could rival those of seasoned musicians, captivated millions worldwide.

Nandi's talents were noticed. She caught the attention of some of the biggest names in music, including the legendary Dave Grohl from the Foo Fighters, who engaged in a drum battle with her. Her triumph in this friendly competition further elevated her status as a musical prodigy.

Nandi Bushell's story is inspiring, reminding us that age is just a number when it comes to achieving greatness. Her confidence, exceptional talent, and passion have made her a role model for aspiring young musicians everywhere. Despite the pressures of early fame, Nandi stays true to her love for music, showcasing that confidence and self-esteem are crucial to navigating life's challenges.

The stories of these four young women illustrate the power of resilience, determination, and the courage to remain true to oneself. They serve as shining examples for girls navigating their path, inspiring them to overcome challenges and pursue their passions with unwavering determination.

# PRACTICAL ADVICE AND TIPS

## Assess the Situation

The first step when facing peer pressure is to pause and take a moment to assess the situation honestly. This means stepping back from the immediacy of the moment to gain a broader perspective. Evaluate the request being made of you—does it align with your personal values, beliefs, and moral compass? If the answer is no, it's essential to consider the potential ramifications of going along with this request. Try to weigh the pros and cons objectively. Ask yourself what you stand to gain versus what you might lose or risk. This analytical approach will provide a firm foundation for making a decision that respects your integrity.

## Stand Your Ground

Mastering the art of assertive communication is another critical skill when dealing with peer pressure. This means learning to clearly and confidently articulate your thoughts, feelings, and beliefs, even when they may not align with those of others. It's important to understand that standing up for yourself is not about being confrontational but about respecting your beliefs while maintaining respect for others. Practice expressing your standpoint respectfully and confidently, reminding yourself that your opinions and feelings are valid and deserving of consideration.

## Seek Support

An essential aspect of managing peer pressure is cultivating a supportive network around you. This means surrounding yourself with positive influences—friends who respect your decisions and share similar values. These individuals can offer encouragement and understanding when facing tough choices. Furthermore, don't hesitate to reach out to trusted adults or mentors in your life. Whether they're parents, teachers, counselors, or other role models, their guidance and perspective can be invaluable when navigating difficult situations. Remember, you're not alone on this journey; some people care about your well-being and are ready to provide the support you need.

## Develop Resilience

Lastly, building resilience is a powerful tool against peer pressure. This skill allows you to adapt and recover from challenging situations with strength and grace. Cultivating resilience involves focusing on your unique strengths and learning how to harness them effectively. It also means practicing self-compassion, understanding that it's okay to make mistakes, and seeing them as opportunities for growth rather than setbacks. Maintaining a positive outlook, even in adversity, is also essential to resilience. This might involve techniques like positive affirmations or mindfulness practices to help keep your spirit buoyant during challenging times.

These four pillars—assessing the situation, standing your ground, seeking support, and developing resilience—provide a comprehensive approach to handling peer pressure. By adopting these strategies, you can navigate the intricacies of social challenges with confidence, self-assurance, and grace.

# WRITING PROMPTS AND REFLECTION QUESTIONS

* Think about a time when you faced peer pressure or a social challenge. How did you handle it? What could you have done differently to navigate the situation more effectively?

* How can you practice assertiveness in your daily life? What are some situations where you could have been more assertive, and how might that have changed the outcome?

* Consider the role models discussed in this chapter (Selena Gomez and Gitanjali Rao). What aspects of their resilience and determination do you admire? How can you apply their lessons to your life?

# KEY TAKEAWAYS

**When facing peer pressure, learn to assess situations and make decisions based on your values and beliefs.**

Learning to assess situations critically and make decisions based on your values and beliefs is fundamental, especially when facing peer pressure. Don't be swayed by the crowd; take the time to understand the situation and evaluate the options based on your values, beliefs, and long-term goals. This way, you are more likely to make choices that you're comfortable with and that reflect who you truly are.

**Practice assertive communication and stand up for yourself and your beliefs with confidence and respect.**

Developing the ability to communicate your thoughts and feelings assertively is essential. This involves expressing yourself openly and honestly while respecting others' perspectives. Stand up for yourself and your beliefs, even when they might be unpopular or face opposition. Remember, your opinions are valid and worthy of being heard. Developing this skill fosters self-confidence and mutual respect in relationships.

**Seek support from positive influences and trusted adults when navigating social challenges.**

As you navigate the complexities of social interactions and relationships, don't hesitate to seek support. Surround yourself with positive influences—friends who respect your decisions and share your values. Reach out to trusted adults, mentors, or counselors when facing difficult situations or when in doubt.

Remember, seeking help is not a sign of weakness but a strength demonstrating your commitment to personal growth.

**Develop resilience by focusing on your strengths, practicing self-compassion, and maintaining a positive outlook.**

Developing resilience is crucial for navigating social challenges effectively. Resilience involves adapting and bouncing back from adversity, disappointment, and failure. Cultivate resilience by focusing on your strengths and achievements, practicing self-compassion when you face setbacks, and maintaining a positive outlook on life. Recognize that challenges are a part of life and are often opportunities for growth and learning. By developing resilience, you will equip yourself with the emotional strength to handle life's challenges gracefully and confidently.

# INTERACTIVE ACTIVITIES AND EXERCISES

* **Role-Playing Scenarios:** Practice navigating challenging social situations by role-playing with a trusted friend or family member. Take turns acting out scenarios involving peer pressure or social challenges, and practice responding assertively and confidently.

* **Resilience Journal:** Create a journal dedicated to documenting your experiences with resilience. Reflect on situations where you've faced challenges and successfully navigated them. Write down the strategies you used, the

lessons you learned, and the strengths you demonstrated. Review your journal regularly to remind yourself of your resilience and ability to overcome obstacles.

# QUOTES TO INSPIRE AND MOTIVATE

"Don't let anyone dull your sparkle."
—UNKNOWN

"In the middle of difficulty lies opportunity."
—ALBERT EINSTEIN

"You have power over your mind, not outside events. Realize this, and you will find strength."
—MARCUS AURELIUS

"The only person you should try to be better than is the person you were yesterday."
—UNKNOWN

# Focus on Role Models

**Selena Gomez:** Selena's openness about her social and mental health struggles showcases her resilience and determination. By discussing her experiences and seeking support, she has inspired others to face their challenges head-on and helped to destigmatize mental health issues.

**Gitanjali Rao:** Gitanjali has exemplified resilience and determination by pursuing her passion for science and innovation despite facing peer pressure and social challenges. Her unwavering dedication to her interests and her ability to stay true to her goals demonstrate the power of perseverance and self-confidence.

**Marsai Martin:** The youngest executive producer in Hollywood, known for her role in the TV show *Black-ish*, Marsai Martin has shown maturity beyond her years in navigating the pressures of the entertainment industry.

**Nandi Bushell:** A young drummer and musician who has played with some of the world's biggest rock bands, Nandi Bushell continues to pursue her passion for music while handling the pressures and expectations that come with fame at a young age.

# RISING ABOVE

As an author and motivational speaker today, I am often asked about my experiences dealing with peer pressure and social challenges. A standout experience from high school has profoundly shaped who I am today.

During the ninth grade, a group of students I was part of in my Spanish class decided to skip school one day. This act was not a tradition but a fleeting rebellion that was viewed as "cool." Regrettably, the chosen day coincided with a crucial science exam that accounted for a large part of our final grade. This unexpected predicament forced me to navigate the challenging terrain of social acceptance and academic responsibility.

I grappled with my decision on the evening before the proposed skip day. The yearning to conform to my peers was intense, yet my commitment to my educational future was equally compelling. After a thoughtful conversation with my parents, I chose to go against the grain, attend school, and take the science exam, resisting the enticing peer pressure.

Arriving at school the next day, I was one of the only students from my group who decided to attend. The hallways were filled with the usual chatter and classroom activities. Yet, whispers of surprise and mockery followed me from those who knew about the skip-day plan. Despite the discomfort, I stood tall. I walked into the examination room with determination and focused on the test before me.

When my peers returned the following day, I felt like the odd one out. I was greeted with a mix of sneers, surprised expressions, and, unexpectedly, a few quiet words of admiration. The repercussions of my decision were temporary. My grades remained robust, and my confidence bolstered.

This unexpected event became a turning point in my life. It underscored the importance of standing up for my beliefs, even when it invites pressure. I learned the value of prioritizing long-term goals over momentary social acceptance. Today, I utilize this experience to inform my decisions and inspire others as they navigate peer pressure and social challenges. My story reminds me that following your unique path is okay, even if it diverges from the crowd.

# DRAWING STRENGTH AND INSPIRATION

As we conclude this illuminating chapter, let's take a moment to reflect on the insights and tools we've gathered to handle peer pressure, cope with social challenges, and cultivate resilience. In our quest for self-confidence and empowerment, we've explored strategies to help us navigate the social situations we encounter through adolescence.

We began by addressing the all-too-common issue of peer pressure. In this section, we armed ourselves with the tools to step back and critically assess situations when they arise. We explored the importance of identifying whether the pressures we face align with our values and beliefs. We also learned the significance of weighing the potential consequences of our actions, thereby encouraging informed decisions that we can stand by with confidence and integrity.

From here, we ventured into the realm of assertiveness, developing our abilities to stand our ground in the face of disagreement or opposition. We discovered that it's not just about holding our position but communicating our thoughts, feelings, and beliefs respectfully and confidently. Through continuous practice, we can become more adept at expressing ourselves and our viewpoints, ensuring our voice is heard and respected.

Next, we underscored the importance of cultivating a network of support. We realized that surrounding ourselves with positive influences and friends who respect our decisions and share our values can provide a sturdy safety net when faced with challenging situations. We also acknowledged the power of reaching out to trusted adults or mentors when we find ourselves in tricky predicaments, appreciating that their wisdom and guidance can provide a different perspective and valuable advice.

Further, we delved into the concept of resilience, understanding how to harness our inner strength to bounce back from adversities and challenges. We learned to celebrate our unique strengths and exercise self-compassion, understanding that mistakes are inevitable and can be transformational stepping stones to growth and learning. Even when things seem bleak, maintaining a positive outlook emerged as a critical component of resilience.

As we learned these practical tips and strategies, we drew inspiration from real-life stories and anecdotes of notable role models like Selena Gomez and Gitanjali Rao. Their journeys illustrated how resilience, determination, and authenticity can guide us through social challenges and peer pressure. Their stories were clear reminders that every challenge we face is an opportunity for growth and self-discovery.

As we turn the page to the next chapter, carry the lessons and strategies gleaned from this one. Always remember to be true to yourself, boldly stand up for your beliefs, and draw inspiration from the lives of our role models. Know, with unshakeable conviction, that you can handle any social challenge with grace, resilience, and unwavering confidence. This chapter was a stepping stone in your journey toward greater self-confidence. This journey continues to unfold with each new day and each new experience.

# CHAPTER 4

## Foster Healthy Relationships

This chapter promises to be a journey of discovery and learning as we explore the significance of fostering and maintaining healthy relationships. We'll be navigating through various facets of relationships—encompassing friendships, familial bonds, and romantic connections—each bringing unique dimensions, challenges, and rewards.

Understanding the importance of healthy relationships is the first step toward cultivating them. These relationships serve as cornerstones in our lives, providing us with emotional support, understanding, companionship, and opportunities for personal growth. These relationships often shape our perspectives, influence our decisions, and contribute significantly to our emotional and mental well-being.

We'll focus on key topics integral to building and maintaining healthy relationships as we traverse the chapter. Communication skills will be at the forefront of our discussion, unraveling the art of expressing our feelings, thoughts, and concerns effectively and empathetically. We'll explore the role of active listening and learn how to build conversations that promote mutual understanding and respect.

Next, we will delve into setting boundaries—a crucial element in any relationship. Establishing boundaries helps to create a healthy sense of self and promotes mutual respect. We'll learn how to assertively define and express our limits, ensuring our needs and feelings are recognized and valued.

The essence of trust in relationships will also be a focal point in our exploration. Trust, the bedrock of any relationship, can build strong connections and foster a safe space for vulnerability and honesty. We'll investigate ways to cultivate and sustain trust, understanding its intricacies in different relationships.

Moreover, we'll discuss the importance of emotional support. We'll understand how to give and receive support, recognizing its role in creating strong, resilient connections. Emotional support fosters empathy and strengthens bonds; being open to receiving it allows vulnerability and growth.

As we navigate these essential topics, we will be inspired by real-life stories from remarkable role models like Michelle Obama and Yara Shahidi. Their experiences and insights will guide us, illuminating our understanding of healthy relationships.

So, let's embark on this enlightening journey to learn, understand, and practice the skills necessary to build and sustain strong, positive relationships in our lives. Get ready to immerse yourself in this wealth of knowledge and enrich your understanding of the integral role that healthy relationships play in our journey to self-confidence and overall well-being. Welcome to Chapter 4 of *The Ultimate Book of Confidence for Teen Girls*!

# REAL-LIFE STORIES

## *Michelle Obama*
### HARNESSING THE POWER OF
### SUPPORTIVE RELATIONSHIPS

Michelle Obama, a former First Lady, acclaimed author, and dedicated advocate, is a shining beacon who underlines the strength of nurturing robust, supportive relationships. Her life's journey is punctuated by an unwavering commitment to maintaining and cherishing the connections that enrich her existence, from her supportive partnership with Barack Obama to her deep bonds with her daughters, Malia and Sasha, and her wide circle of friends.

Born and raised on the South Side of Chicago, Michelle was influenced by her close-knit family who instilled in her the values of hard work and education from a young age. This early familial support and encouragement undeniably played a significant role in shaping her success.

Her relationship with her husband, Barack Obama, is another testament to the power of a supportive partnership. Together, they navigated the challenges of raising a family in the public eye, dealing with intense scrutiny and pressure. Their mutual respect, open communication, and shared values have kept their bond strong and allowed them to support each other through various personal and professional milestones.

Beyond her immediate family, Michelle has also nurtured a strong network of friendships. Her friends have provided her emotional support, companionship, and shared experiences, contributing significantly to her growth. Michelle's relentless dedication to cultivating and preserving these healthy relationships is a powerful testament to the positive impact such connections can have on our lives.

## *Yara Shahidi*

## CELEBRATING THE VALUE OF FAMILY, FRIENDS, AND MENTORS

Remember Yara Shahidi from our first chapter? This accomplished actress, burgeoning activist, and passionate advocate for education and social justice highlights the importance of building and maintaining meaningful relationships in shaping one's life journey. Her success story is a beautiful tapestry woven together by the healthy relationships she's nurtured with her family, friends, and mentors.

Yara's family plays a fundamental role in her life. She often acknowledges their unwavering support as a driving force behind her success. Her family encouraged her acting career and instilled in her a deep sense of responsibility toward social issues, shaping her into the influential activist she is today.

Her robust relationships extend beyond her family. Yara has established strong bonds with mentors within the entertainment industry, including industry veterans and peers who have provided invaluable advice, guidance, and inspiration throughout her career. These relationships have proven crucial in her personal and professional growth, paving her path to success.

Moreover, her friendships, whether within or outside the entertainment industry, have provided her with emotional support and companionship, contributing to her overall well-being and sense of self. Yara's story showcases how diverse, supportive relationships can be instrumental in achieving personal and professional goals.

# Billie Eilish
## STAYING TRUE TO YOURSELF AMID STARDOM

Billie Eilish Pirate Baird O'Connell, better known as Billie Eilish, is a testament to maintaining authenticity and fostering healthy relationships amidst the intense pressures of the global music industry. A multiple Grammy award-winning artist, Billie's unique musical style and mature lyrical themes have resonated with a worldwide audience, propelling her to international stardom at a young age.

Born and raised in Los Angeles, Billie was homeschooled alongside her older brother Finneas O'Connell, who became her main collaborator in music. The close relationship between Billie and Finneas was instrumental in shaping her sound and career. Together, they created music in their childhood home, maintaining a creative synergy rooted in mutual respect and shared experiences. This healthy working relationship has undoubtedly been a cornerstone of her success.

Even as her fame skyrocketed, Billie managed to maintain a strong connection with her family, who continues to provide her with emotional support and guidance. Billie's authentic portrayal of her experiences and emotions in her music and her willingness to openly discuss mental health have fostered a strong bond with her fans.

Billie Eilish's story is one of authenticity, resilience, and the power of healthy relationships. It shows us that maintaining strong and supportive connections can be a source of strength and stability amidst success and stardom.

## *Kiara Nirghin*

## THE POWER OF COLLABORATION IN INNOVATION

Kiara Nirghin is a South African inventor known for her innovation in science at a remarkably young age. Her story highlights the importance of fostering healthy relationships in achieving professional goals.

Kiara's interest in science led her to make significant strides in addressing real-world problems. At sixteen, she won the Google Science Fair's Community Impact Award for the Middle East and Africa with her project "No More Thirsty Crops." Her invention, a superabsorbent polymer made from orange peels that can help the soil retain water, has the potential to significantly impact drought-stricken areas.

Kiara's success is not just a result of her inventive prowess but also her ability to foster healthy relationships with her mentors and peers. Her collaborative approach to problem-solving was pivotal in her journey. From seeking advice and feedback to working with others on projects, she recognizes the value of diverse perspectives in innovation.

Kiara's healthy relationships in her professional sphere have helped in her personal growth and served as an example for other young innovators. Her story demonstrates that fostering and maintaining healthy relationships is essential to pursuing one's goals.

These inspiring stories illuminate the immense value of cultivating healthy, supportive relationships amidst peer pressure and career challenges. Their experiences underscore how such relationships can significantly contribute to our personal growth, self-confidence, and success, providing emotional sustenance and practical support as we navigate our unique journeys.

# PRACTICAL ADVICE AND TIPS

## Cultivate the Art of Communication

The importance of effective communication in maintaining and strengthening relationships cannot be overstated. This involves more than just conveying your thoughts and feelings; it requires a willingness to truly listen to what others say. Engage in active listening, paying full attention to the speaker, showing empathy, and offering thoughtful responses. This encourages an environment of mutual respect and understanding. Additionally, express your thoughts and feelings clearly and respectfully, fostering open and honest communication.

Mastering these communication skills is vital to nurturing healthier, more fulfilling relationships.

## Establish and Respect Boundaries

Personal boundaries are essential in every relationship as they define where one person ends and another begins. They help to protect your mental, emotional, and physical well-being. Understanding your limits and communicating these boundaries to those around you is essential. Similarly, it's crucial to respect the boundaries set by others. This mutual recognition and respect for personal boundaries foster healthier relationships and create an environment of mutual respect and understanding.

## Build Trust and Provide Emotional Support

Trust is the cornerstone of all relationships. It's built over time through consistent actions demonstrating reliability, honesty, and support. Make a concerted effort to be someone others can rely on; be honest in your dealings and offer support when needed. Similarly, emotional support plays a significant role in fostering stronger bonds. Be there for your friends and loved ones in times of need. Listen empathetically, offer comforting words, and reassure them they are not alone. Similarly, don't hesitate to seek emotional support when you need it. Remember, being vulnerable and leaning on others for help is okay.

# *Nurture Your Connections*

Relationships need nurturing to grow and thrive. Invest time and effort into maintaining your relationships. Regularly show your loved ones that you value their presence in your life. This could be as simple as sending a text to check in, scheduling regular catch-ups, or expressing appreciation for them. Engage in activities that you enjoy together to strengthen your bonds and create shared memories. These actions show your commitment to the relationship and help to build deeper, more fulfilling connections.

By putting these practical tips into action, you can significantly enhance the quality of your relationships, making them more fulfilling and resilient. Remember, healthy relationships are two-way streets and require effort from both sides. However, the emotional support, companionship, and personal growth they provide make them worth the investment. As we've seen through the inspiring stories of Michelle Obama and Yara Shahidi, nurturing strong, supportive relationships can profoundly impact your personal and professional life, empowering you to achieve your goals with confidence.

# WRITING PROMPTS AND REFLECTION QUESTIONS

* Think about your current relationships (family, friends, romantic partners). How do you practice effective communication, set boundaries, and build trust within these relationships?

* Reflect on a time when you faced a challenge within a relationship. How did you handle the situation, and what lessons did you learn?

* How can you apply the lessons from the role models in this chapter to nurture your relationships and foster personal growth?

# KEY TAKEAWAYS

**Practice effective communication by actively listening and expressing your thoughts and feelings clearly and respectfully.**

Practicing effective communication is a cornerstone of healthy relationships. This involves actively listening when others speak, showing empathy, and expressing your thoughts and feelings clearly and respectfully. Remember, communication is a two-way street, and understanding others' perspectives is as important as sharing your own. By enhancing your communication skills, you will be better able to understand

and be understood, fostering deeper connections with those around you.

**Set personal boundaries and respect the boundaries of others to foster mutual respect within your relationships.**

Personal boundaries are an essential component of all relationships. They help to define your identity, protect your self-esteem, and manage your time and energy effectively. Learn to establish your boundaries and communicate them clearly to others. Equally important is recognizing and respecting the boundaries set by others. Respecting boundaries fosters mutual respect and understanding, ensuring all parties feel comfortable and valued.

**Build trust and offer emotional support within your relationships by being reliable, honest, and supportive.**

Trust is the bedrock of any relationship, and it's built through consistency, reliability, honesty, and transparency. Be dependable, keep your promises, and be honest, even when difficult. Additionally, offering emotional support to those around you and seeking help when needed are key to building strong, resilient relationships. Remember, it's okay to be vulnerable and share your feelings with those you trust.

**Nurture your connections by making time for the people you care about and engaging in activities that strengthen your bonds.**

Our relationships are like gardens—they need regular care and nurturing to thrive. Make time for the people you care about and show them you value their presence. This can involve simple actions like catching up over coffee, sending a thoughtful text, or doing activities you enjoy together. Nurturing your connections strengthens your relationships and contributes to your happiness and well-being.

# INTERACTIVE ACTIVITIES AND EXERCISES

* **Role-Playing Scenarios:** Practice communication and boundary-setting skills by role-playing with a trusted friend or family member. Take turns acting out scenarios involving challenging conversations or situations where boundaries must be established.

* **Relationship Map:** Create a visual representation of your relationships, including family, friends, and romantic connections. Reflect on each relationship's strengths and areas for improvement and brainstorm ways to nurture these connections.

# QUOTES TO INSPIRE
# AND MOTIVATE

"Surround yourself with only people who are going to lift you higher."

—OPRAH WINFREY

"The best thing to hold onto in life is each other."

—AUDREY HEPBURN

"The greatest gift of life is friendship, and I have received it."

—HUBERT H. HUMPHREY

"Family is not an important thing. It's everything."

—MICHAEL J. FOX

# Focus on Role Models

**Michelle Obama:** Michelle's emphasis on the importance of strong, supportive relationships showcases their impact on our lives. Her dedication to her family and friends, and her work as a public servant and advocate, serves as an inspiring example of the power of healthy relationships in fostering personal growth.

**Yara Shahidi:** Yara's journey as an actress and activist highlights the value of fostering healthy relationships with family, friends, and mentors. Her close connections with her family and strong bonds with mentors in the entertainment industry exemplify the power of supportive relationships in achieving personal and professional goals.

**Billie Eilish:** As a world-renowned singer-songwriter, Billie Eilish's relationship with her brother and collaborator, Finneas, is a testament to the importance of fostering healthy relationships. Their bond, professional collaboration, and mutual respect are significant to her success.

**Kiara Nirghin:** A young scientist from South Africa, Kiara's collaborative efforts in her scientific pursuits highlight her ability to foster healthy professional relationships. Her teamwork in science projects has been instrumental in her success, demonstrating the power of cooperation and mutual respect in achieving common goals.

# THE POWER OF CONNECTION

Years ago, during my freshman year of college, I struggled with loneliness and isolation. Having moved halfway across the country to a place where I knew no one, making friends felt daunting.

One day, sitting alone in the cafeteria, I spotted another student sitting alone. Gathering my courage, I decided to approach her. Anna was her name; she was a freshman feeling just as lost and lonely as I was. This common struggle brought us together and began a beautiful friendship.

As our friendship grew, I realized the importance of communication in maintaining healthy relationships. We communicated openly and honestly, whether about the latest college gossip, our struggles, or our dreams for the future. We set boundaries when needed, respected each other's personal space and time, and supported each other during stressful times.

Additionally, we nurtured our connection by spending quality time together. Whether studying for an exam, taking spontaneous road trips, or simply grabbing a coffee between classes, these shared experiences strengthened our bond and created lasting memories.

My friendship with Anna taught me valuable lessons about the power of healthy relationships. It's not just about being there for the fun times but also about offering emotional support and understanding during difficult times. It taught me about respect, communication, and the importance of nurturing connections.

Even though we live in different cities today, Anna and I maintain our strong friendship. The lessons I learned from this relationship have helped me build and maintain other healthy relationships. This experience taught me that fostering healthy relationships requires effort, respect, and a lot of heart. Still, the reward—a lifelong connection with someone who truly understands and supports you—is priceless.

# HEALTHY RELATIONSHIPS AS THE BEDROCK OF CONFIDENCE

Our journey through this chapter has been illuminating, focusing on the significant role that healthy relationships, encompassing friendships, family, and romantic connections, play in our lives. Relationships can be a source of strength, solace, growth, and happiness, contributing to our well-being and self-confidence.

We've explored the key components of healthy relationships in-depth. Open communication, clear boundaries, trust, and emotional support are not just abstract concepts but the foundational building blocks of strong, positive connections. We've learned practical advice and actionable tips on cultivating these essential qualities in our relationships.

Communication skills are crucial in building understanding and fostering a sense of connection. We've discovered how active listening, expressing our feelings respectfully, and encouraging open dialogue can significantly enhance the quality of our relationships.

Boundaries, often overlooked, have been brought into the spotlight. Establishing and respecting personal boundaries ensures mutual respect and promotes healthier, more balanced relationships. Understanding and communicating our limits can protect our well-being and increase our confidence.

Trust, a fundamental pillar of any relationship, was explored in detail. We learned trust can be built and maintained through consistent, reliable, and honest actions. We also delved into the importance of emotional support in strengthening bonds and fostering resilience within our relationships.

Furthermore, we examined the need to invest time and effort into nurturing our connections. Prioritizing the people we care about, participating in shared activities, and creating lasting memories together can deepen our bonds and enhance the quality of our relationships.

Our journey was enriched by the inspiring real-life stories of role models like Michelle Obama and Yara Shahidi. These influential women demonstrated the power of supportive relationships in fostering personal growth, achieving goals, and navigating life's challenges. Their stories illuminated how prioritizing healthy relationships can serve as a driving force toward success and fulfillment.

As we draw this chapter to a close, let's remember the pivotal role relationships play in our journey toward self-confidence and overall success. The lessons we've learned are applicable in the present and will continue to be relevant as we grow and navigate different stages of our lives. Our relationships can be our most significant support and strength, enabling us to overcome hurdles and reach our fullest potential.

As you continue your journey toward greater self-confidence, carry these lessons forward. Prioritize open and honest communication, establish and respect personal boundaries, build and maintain trust, offer and seek emotional support, and invest time and effort in nurturing relationships.

You create a robust foundation for personal growth, happiness, and success by fostering healthy, supportive relationships. Remember, these relationships can be your lifelines, sources of inspiration, and pillars of strength. They can bolster your self-confidence and empower you to navigate life's challenges with resilience and grace.

As we turn the page on this chapter, let's take these insights to heart and strive to build stronger, healthier relationships that uplift us, nurture our growth, and contribute to our journey of becoming more confident, resilient, and successful.

# CHAPTER 5

## Cultivate a Positive Body Image

Chapter 5 focuses on creating a positive body image and developing a healthy relationship with your body. In today's world, we are frequently confronted with an onslaught of unrealistic beauty standards. These standards, often perpetuated by media and societal influences, can have a profound impact, leading to negative body image and erosion of self-esteem, particularly among young girls.

This chapter aims to tackle this challenging issue head-on. We'll dive deep into integral subjects such as body positivity, the art of self-acceptance, understanding the pervasive impact of media influence, and the importance of self-care. Each area plays a pivotal role in how we perceive ourselves and navigate the world around us.

Body positivity is a movement that advocates for the acceptance of all bodies regardless of physical ability, size, gender, race, or appearance. It's about celebrating body diversity, challenging societal norms, and promoting self-love and respect for all bodies.

Understanding self-acceptance involves embracing your whole self—your strengths, your weaknesses, and everything in between. It means valuing yourself without conditions or reservations and seeing yourself through a lens of compassion and understanding.

Media influence can shape our perceptions of beauty and self-worth in significant ways. We'll discuss how to critically engage with media, understand its impacts, and cultivate a resilient mindset that celebrates your unique beauty instead of comparing yourself with unrealistic standards.

The practice of self-care goes beyond merely indulging in pampering sessions. It's about respecting your body, nourishing it with healthy food, keeping it active, giving it the rest it needs, and listening to its signals.

Through real-life stories and inspiring anecdotes from role models like Ashley Graham and Marsai Martin, we aim to illuminate the pathway to positive body image and self-love. Ashley, a plus-size model, and Marsai, a young actress and producer, have consistently championed body positivity and self-acceptance in their respective spheres. Their journeys offer practical insights and inspiring lessons for teen girls navigating similar challenges.

Chapter 5 is not just a mere compilation of advice and tips. It's an empowering journey toward self-love and acceptance, designed to equip you with the necessary tools to cultivate a positive body image, no matter the societal pressures you may face. As we embark on this enlightening journey, let's celebrate our bodies, embrace our unique beauty, and nurture our self-confidence. After all, our bodies are unique, and they deserve nothing but love and respect.

# REAL-LIFE STORIES

## Ashley Graham

## SHATTERING STEREOTYPES AND PROMOTING BODY POSITIVITY

Ashley Graham, a Nebraska-born model, entrepreneur, and body positivity advocate, has made it her life's mission to break barriers in the fashion industry and inspire women around the world to embrace their bodies, no matter their shape or size. Her transformative journey through the notoriously exclusivist world of fashion modeling is a testament to her courage, determination, and unwavering commitment to challenging societal beauty standards.

Ashley refused to conform to the industry's restrictive norms despite early rejection and criticism due to her size. Instead, she turned her struggles into a platform for advocating body positivity. Her resolve and tenacity made her one of the first plus-sized models to appear on the covers of prestigious magazines like *Vogue*, *Elle*, and *Sports Illustrated*, making her an industry trailblazer.

Beyond her accomplishments as a model, Ashley's influence is particularly evident in her advocacy work. She champions that beauty is not confined to a specific size or shape and encourages women to confidently embrace their bodies. Her candid discussions about her experiences with body image, self-esteem, and the pressures of societal expectations have sparked necessary conversations about body positivity.

Furthermore, Ashley uses her entrepreneurial prowess to create inclusive lingerie and clothing lines to celebrate all bodies, reinforcing her commitment to promoting body positivity. She also mentors young models, using her experiences to guide and support them in navigating the industry.

Ashley Graham's journey is a powerful reminder that our physical appearance does not define our self-worth. Her story inspires women worldwide to celebrate their bodies, challenge societal norms, and confidently embrace their unique beauty. In breaking barriers and advocating body positivity, Ashley has shown that change is possible when we stay true to our authentic selves and stand against societal expectations.

## Marsai Martin's
## GRACEFUL RESPONSE TO ONLINE CRITICISM

Marsai Martin, the young actress and producer, exemplifies resilience and confidence. She faced a challenging situation when she was subjected to negative comments about her appearance during an awards show. The incident could have easily discouraged her; however, Marsai responded with elegance and self-assuredness, setting an example for young girls everywhere. Instead of allowing the criticism to lower her self-esteem, Marsai took it in stride, demonstrating that a person's value does not lie in others' opinions but in their self-acceptance. Marsai's commitment to promoting body positivity shines through her actions and words. Her story teaches us that the power to define our beauty and worth lies within us, and we should not let external negativity influence our self-image.

*Lizzo*

# UNAPOLOGETIC AUTHENTICITY AND BODY POSITIVITY

Born Melissa Viviane Jefferson, Lizzo is an American singer, rapper, and flutist who has emerged as a powerful force in the music industry. She is known for her electrifying performances and soulful music. Lizzo's impact extends beyond her artistry to her unapologetic advocacy for body positivity and self-love.

Lizzo's journey to stardom wasn't easy; she faced numerous rejections and criticisms because of her size. However, she never let societal expectations define her. Instead, she used these obstacles to fuel her music and advocate for body positivity.

Her songs often carry powerful messages about self-love, acceptance, and body positivity. Her music and platform encourage her fans to embrace their bodies and feel comfortable in their skin, regardless of societal pressures.

Lizzo's unwavering self-confidence and authenticity make her a beacon of body positivity. She is a testament to the power of embracing one's unique beauty and living unapologetically. Lizzo's journey shows us that when we break away from societal expectations and love ourselves, we can achieve greatness and inspire others to do the same.

# *Iskra Lawrence*
## REDEFINING BEAUTY STANDARDS
## AND INSPIRING BODY CONFIDENCE

Iskra Lawrence, a British model and body positivity advocate, has challenged societal norms about beauty and promoting body confidence. Born and raised in Worcestershire, England, Iskra embarked on her modeling career at an early age. However, she faced rejection because her body didn't fit the industry's narrow beauty standards.

Rather than succumb to these pressures, Iskra chose to challenge them. She pioneered promoting unretouched photos, pushing for more diverse and realistic representations of women in the media. Her work has sparked necessary conversations about body image, self-esteem, and the fashion industry's impact on these issues.

Beyond modeling, Iskra has dedicated herself to body positivity advocacy. She is an ambassador for the National Eating Disorders Association; she shared her experiences to raise awareness about the realities of body image struggles and eating disorders. Additionally, Iskra has used her platform to create the "everyBODY with Iskra" initiative. This inclusive fitness program emphasizes health and well-being over size and shape.

Her candidness in discussing her struggles and commitment to breaking down beauty stereotypes make Iskra an inspiring role model for women globally. Through her work, she encourages others to embrace their bodies, love their unique beauty, and challenge societal norms.

Iskra Lawrence's journey is a powerful testament to the impact of cultivating body positivity and challenging the status quo. Her determination to redefine beauty standards, promote body confidence, and inspire others to do the same demonstrates the power of embracing one's unique beauty and rejecting societal expectations. By doing so, she empowers others to feel comfortable in their skin. She continues to break down barriers and drive change within the fashion industry.

These powerful narratives serve as an inspiration for all teen girls navigating their journeys toward self-love and positive body image. Through their personal experiences, Ashley Graham, Marsai Martin, Lizzo, and Iskra Lawrence show us the value of resilience, self-confidence, and a strong sense of self-worth in the face of societal pressures and criticism. They leveraged their platforms to drive the conversation around body positivity. By embracing their unique bodies and challenging societal norms, they inspire countless individuals worldwide to do the same and contribute significantly to a broader societal shift toward accepting and celebrating all bodies. Their journeys remind us that we all have the power to redefine beauty standards and shape a more inclusive and accepting world.

# PRACTICAL ADVICE AND TIPS

## Embrace Self-Acceptance Wholeheartedly

Your first step toward cultivating a positive body image is practicing self-acceptance. This means fully embracing your unique body—its shape, size, and appearance. Your body is your own, unlike any other, and that uniqueness should be celebrated. Recognize that your body is a dynamic entity, constantly changing and evolving. Puberty, aging, and life experiences will influence your physical appearance; these changes are a natural part of life. It's important to understand that everyone has unique qualities and features that make them beautiful in their own way.

## Be Mindful of the Media You Consume

In the age of digital media, we are constantly bombarded with images that often portray unrealistic and unattainable beauty standards. It's vital to be critical of the media you consume and to remember that many photos are manipulated or enhanced to represent these standards. Surround yourself with positive role models, both online and offline, who advocate for body diversity and self-acceptance. Engaging with uplifting and authentic representations of beauty can significantly impact your self-perception and self-worth.

## Prioritize Self-Care

Your relationship with your body isn't just about how you perceive it; it's also about how you treat it. Prioritizing self-care is an essential part of fostering a positive body image. This can include engaging in activities that make you feel good about yourself and your body, such as regular exercise, nourishing your body with a balanced diet, ensuring you get adequate sleep, and taking time to relax and unwind. Self-care is about treating your body with kindness and respect, acknowledging its needs, and taking steps to meet them.

## Celebrate Your Body's Capabilities

Often, we focus so much on appearance that we forget to appreciate the incredible things our bodies are capable of. Whether running, dancing, painting, writing, or simply carrying you through your day, your body is a marvel. Instead of obsessing over how it looks, try shifting your focus to what it can do. This shift in perspective can foster a more profound sense of appreciation and respect for your body, contributing to a more positive body image.

These practical strategies offer a roadmap to developing a healthier relationship with your body. You can foster positive body image and self-esteem by embracing self-acceptance, being critical of the media, prioritizing self-care, and appreciating your body's capabilities. This journey toward self-love and acceptance isn't always easy, but it's worthwhile.

Remember, you are unique, and your beauty is incomparable.
Embrace it.

# WRITING PROMPTS AND REFLECTION QUESTIONS

* Reflect on a time when you felt self-conscious about your body. What contributed to those feelings? How did you cope with them?

* List three things you love about your body and consider how they contribute to your unique beauty.

* How can you challenge unrealistic beauty standards in your life? What actions can you take to promote body positivity and self-acceptance?

# KEY TAKEAWAYS

**Embrace your unique body shape, size, and appearance.**

Every body is unique, and this uniqueness should be embraced and celebrated. Your body shape, size, and appearance are part of what makes you *you*. Try to focus on what you love about yourself and appreciate your body for what it can do. This isn't always easy in a world that often promotes narrow beauty standards, but remember, real beauty is about being authentically you.

**Limit exposure to unrealistic beauty standards and focus on positive role models.**

Media can often portray unrealistic and homogeneous beauty standards that can negatively impact your self-image. Be aware of this influence and consider limiting your exposure to such media. Instead, surround yourself with positive role models and messages celebrating diverse body types and appearances. Remember, images in the media are often manipulated and fail to represent the diversity and beauty of real bodies.

**Engage in self-care and prioritize activities that make you feel good about yourself.**

Taking care of your body is essential to self-love and body positivity. This means engaging in activities that nourish your body and make you feel good about yourself. This could be exercising regularly, eating nutritious food, getting adequate sleep, or simply relaxing and unwinding. Treating your body kindly and respectfully promotes a positive body image and well-being.

**Appreciate the incredible things your body is capable of.**

Instead of focusing on your body's appearance, focus on what your body can do. Your body is an incredible machine that carries you through each day, enabling you to run, dance, laugh, hug, and much more. Acknowledging and celebrating these capabilities can help foster a positive body image and more profound gratitude and appreciation for your body.

# INTERACTIVE ACTIVITIES AND EXERCISES

* **Create a body positivity collage:** Collect images, quotes, and phrases that promote body diversity and self-acceptance. Display your collage in a place where you'll see it daily as a reminder to love and appreciate your body.

* **Affirmations:** Write down positive affirmations about your body and appearance. Repeat these affirmations daily to boost your confidence and self-love.

# QUOTES TO INSPIRE AND MOTIVATE

"You are imperfect, permanently and inevitably flawed. And you are beautiful."

—AMY BLOOM

"To be beautiful means to be yourself. You don't need to be accepted by others. You need to accept yourself."

—THICH NH T HANH

"Your body is an instrument, not an ornament."

—GLENNON DOYLE

# Focus on Role Models

**Ashley Graham:** By breaking barriers in the fashion industry and advocating for body positivity, Ashley Graham demonstrates the importance of embracing one's body and feeling confident in one's skin, regardless of size or shape.

**Marsai Martin:** As a young actress and producer, Marsai Martin's resilience in the face of criticism and dedication to promoting body positivity inspire young girls to feel confident in their skin and embrace their unique beauty.

**Lizzo:** Born Melissa Viviane Jefferson, Lizzo is an American singer, rapper, and flutist who has won numerous awards for her music. Lizzo has been vocal about body positivity and self-love, using her platform to inspire her fans to embrace their bodies and feel comfortable in their skin.

**Iskra Lawrence:** A British model and body positivity advocate, Iskra Lawrence actively challenges societal norms about beauty and encourages young girls to love and accept their bodies as they are.

# FINDING BEAUTY WITHIN

I was always heavier than my peers in my teenage years and struggled with persistent acne. The comments and sideways glances did not escape my notice, nor did the radiant, smooth-skinned models in every magazine and billboard. Those images felt like a constant reminder of how far I was from the societal standards of beauty.

My self-esteem plummeted, and I became hyper-aware of my size and skin. I felt my body and face were barriers preventing me from fitting in rather than parts of who I am. These perceived imperfections felt like they overshadowed my abilities and qualities.

Everything changed when I stumbled upon a dance class in my local community center. Despite being out of my comfort zone, I was captivated by the rhythm and energy. The prospect of joining was terrifying at first, but something about the raw and freeing expression through movement was irresistible.

To say I was a clumsy dancer would be an understatement. I often missed beats, forgot the choreography, and fell out of sync with the class. But with every misstep, I began to experience a decisive shift in perspective.

Instead of dwelling on my size, I marveled at the strength and resilience of my body. It could sustain long dance sessions, recover, and be ready to twirl and sway again the next day. I felt powerful, and this feeling replaced the constant criticism in my head.

On the other hand, my acne, which I had tried to hide with layers of makeup, seemed less significant over time. I noticed that the people I admired were cherished for their kindness, resilience, humor, and other qualities that had nothing to do with appearance.

One day, while dancing in front of the mirror, I caught a glimpse of myself—sweaty, smiling, and lost in the rhythm of the music. I was not the flawless model in a magazine, but I was glowing with joy and confidence. This was a new reflection I was not used to but was eager to embrace.

This marked the beginning of my journey toward body positivity. I began acknowledging my body's ability and potential rather than criticizing it for its appearance. I learned to accept my skin, knowing that acne didn't define my worth or beauty.

My path to self-acceptance and body positivity has been a curve. I still have days filled with doubts and insecurities, but I've learned to dance through them, one step at a time. The more I dance, the more I appreciate the strength, resilience, and beauty in every pound, every pimple, and, most importantly, in myself.

# EMBRACING POSITIVE BODY IMAGE AND SELF-LOVE

In Chapter 5, we've critically explored a topic that affects all of us but is often overlooked—cultivating a positive body image and fostering a healthy relationship with our bodies.

In a world often riddled with unrealistic beauty standards and negative media influences, learning to embrace and appreciate our unique bodies is essential to our journey toward self-confidence and self-love.

We've delved into crucial areas such as body positivity, self-acceptance, the influence of media, and the role of self-care in nurturing a positive perception of ourselves. By providing practical advice and actionable tips, we've aimed to equip you with valuable tools to help you navigate your journey toward positive body image. These include practicing self-acceptance, critically analyzing media representation, engaging in self-care routines that honor and respect your body, and celebrating your body's remarkable capabilities.

Reflection and introspection are also crucial elements of this journey, and we've introduced pertinent reflection questions and suggested activities designed to stimulate more profound understanding and self-awareness. These tools are meant to guide you in understanding your current relationship with your body, identifying areas that might need attention, and developing strategies for improving your body image.

This chapter is only complete with inspiring real-life stories and anecdotes from powerful role models like Ashley Graham and Marsai Martin. These extraordinary women have publicly embraced their unique bodies and spoken about their journeys toward body positivity and self-acceptance, inspiring countless others. Their stories prove that confidence, resilience, and self-love can thrive in the face of societal pressures and criticism.

In conclusion, remember that your body is unique, powerful, and beautiful just the way it is. It serves you daily, allowing you to experience the world and engage with the people and activities you love. Your body deserves respect, love, and appreciation. Remember to carry these lessons with you as you continue your journey toward self-confidence. By fostering a positive body image, you will cultivate self-love and confidence that will serve you now and throughout your life. Embrace your body, celebrate your individuality, and know that you are enough, just as you are.

# CHAPTER 6

# Manage Stress and Anxiety

Adolescence is often likened to a rollercoaster—a whirlwind of emotions and experiences that can be both thrilling and overwhelming. During these formative years, you may encounter challenges and changes that test your resilience and adaptability. Along with the excitement of growth and discovery, adolescence can bring stress, anxiety, and other mental health concerns. Recognizing this, we must understand how to manage these challenges effectively, ensuring our mental well-being is never sidelined.

Chapter 6 will delve deeper into strategies for managing stress, alleviating anxiety, and prioritizing mental well-being during this significant phase of life. Our objective is to equip you with the tools and techniques to navigate these turbulent times with confidence and grace, maintaining your mental health equilibrium.

Our discussion will revolve around vital topics such as effective stress management, the role of mindfulness in mental well-being, various coping strategies to tackle anxiety and stress, and the crucial aspect of self-care. Stress management will address techniques to help you identify stressors and devise strategies to manage them effectively. The segment on mindfulness will explore how staying present and fully engaged in the current moment can contribute significantly to mental peace and balance.

Further, we will explore various coping strategies for facing challenging situations. This can include everything from relaxation techniques and deep breathing exercises to cognitive strategies like reframing negative thoughts. The segment on self-care will reinforce the importance of looking after your mental and emotional well-being through rest, recreation, and maintaining healthy social connections.

As we journey through these topics, we'll also draw inspiration from individuals who've used their platforms to spotlight mental health issues. One such individual is the acclaimed actress Emma Stone. Emma has openly shared her experiences with anxiety, thus contributing to the critical conversation about mental health and helping to lessen the stigma often associated with it. Her story provides a valuable reminder that mental health challenges do not discriminate and that it's okay to seek help.

This chapter invites you to understand and prioritize your mental well-being. It will underscore that mental health is just as important as physical health, and learning to manage stress and anxiety during adolescence can set the stage for a healthier, more balanced adult life. Let's embark on this journey together, fostering a better understanding of our minds and cultivating strategies for well-being that will serve us both during adolescence and into the future.

# REAL-LIFE STORIES

## *Emma Stone's*

## BRAVE JOURNEY WITH ANXIETY:
## A VOICE FOR MENTAL HEALTH

Emma Stone, an Oscar-winning actress and influential advocate for mental health, has been remarkably transparent about her journey with anxiety. Born Emily Jean Stone, the Arizona native first grappled with severe anxiety and debilitating panic attacks as a child. This daunting experience, although challenging, did not define her or confine her ambitions. Instead, it fueled her journey of self-discovery and resilience.

From her early childhood, Emma employed various strategies to comprehend and manage her anxiety. Therapy played a crucial role in this journey, providing a sanctuary for her to express her feelings candidly and offering a professional perspective on navigating her emotions. These sessions equipped her with valuable coping mechanisms and a deeper understanding of her mental health, which she carries with her today.

In addition to therapy, Emma embraced mindfulness practices like meditation. This technique helped her stay grounded and focused on the present moment, which is crucial to quelling anxious thoughts and maintaining a sense of calm in turbulent times. Such practices serve as valuable tools in her arsenal to combat anxiety, showcasing the importance of holistic approaches in managing mental health.

Interestingly, Emma's journey with anxiety intersected with her passion for acting. The stage, in many ways, provided a therapeutic outlet for her. It allowed her to channel her emotions constructively, explore various facets of the human experience, and find solace in the universality of the emotions portrayed. This form of artistic expression served as a potent form of therapy itself, contributing significantly to her mental well-being.

However, Emma's story transcends her personal experiences. Fearlessly sharing her struggles has sparked crucial conversations about mental health on public platforms, breaking down societal stigmas. She has used her influential status to normalize mental health discussions, encouraging others to seek support and prioritize their well-being.

Emma Stone's journey is a testament to resilience, an inspiring story of turning personal struggles into sources of strength. It is a compelling reminder that, despite the challenges mental health issues present, they do not diminish one's worth or potential. Emma's bravery serves as an enduring beacon of hope for those grappling with similar problems, underscoring the message that it's okay not to be okay, and more importantly, that help is available and progress is achievable.

## Jazz Jennings
## A BEACON FOR TRANSGENDER YOUTH

Jazz Jennings, a vibrant young woman, LGBTQ+ rights activist, and reality television star, has been a pivotal voice for transgender youth, breaking barriers and fostering understanding. Born male but identifying as female from the age of five, Jazz's journey was unconventional and fraught with challenges. However, her remarkable strength and resilience have been her guiding forces.

With the unwavering support of her family, Jazz began her transition at a young age, making her one of the youngest publicly documented individuals to identify as transgender. This early visibility catapulted her into the public eye, leading her to use her platform to educate others about transgender experiences. She coauthored a children's book, *I Am Jazz*, to promote understanding and acceptance of transgender youth, which later inspired a TLC reality show of the same name.

Beyond her creative projects, Jazz actively advocates for transgender rights. She is one of the founders of the TransKids Purple Rainbow Foundation, an organization dedicated to supporting transgender youth. Her efforts extend to public speaking engagements, where she shares her experiences to increase visibility and understanding of transgender issues.

Her honest portrayal of her transition journey, both its highs and lows, through her reality show has made her a household name. But more importantly, it has given visibility to the often overlooked and misunderstood transgender community.

Jazz Jennings' journey is one of courage, acceptance, and unwavering authenticity. Her story inspires and educates, sending a powerful message about embracing one's true self regardless of societal expectations and norms.

# Hailee Steinfeld

## RISING ABOVE ANXIETY

Hailee Steinfeld, an award-winning actress and successful pop artist, has shown tremendous grace in managing her career's stress and anxiety. Hailee stepped into the limelight at a young age with her breakthrough role in the movie *True Grit*, earning her an Academy Award nomination when she was only fourteen. This early success thrust her into an industry often associated with immense pressure and high expectations.

However, Hailee has navigated her way with admirable composure and resilience. She has been open about her experiences with stress and anxiety, setting an example for many young people dealing with similar issues. Recognizing the importance of mental health, Hailee has employed various strategies to keep her anxiety at bay. She often talks about the benefits of exercise, maintaining a balanced diet, and the importance of taking personal time for relaxation and mindfulness activities.

In addition to her proactive approach toward her mental health, Steinfeld emphasizes the importance of a robust support system. Her family has been her rock, providing emotional stability in the face of Hollywood's often tumultuous nature.

Hailee's successful navigation of her career stress and public discourse about mental health issues make her an important role model for young people worldwide. Her journey underscores that it's okay to acknowledge our struggles and seek help when needed, providing a comforting reminder that we are not alone in our battles with anxiety.

# Overcoming Test Anxiety

## SARAH'S STORY

High school student Sarah experienced debilitating anxiety leading up to exams, a common situation known as test anxiety. The anticipation of the exams, the pressure to perform, and the fear of failing overwhelmed her, often resulting in poor performance despite her efforts. Test anxiety manifested in physical symptoms like headaches and stomachaches and psychological symptoms like restlessness and panic, which further hindered her performance. Recognizing the toll this was taking on her academic performance and overall well-being, Sarah decided to take steps to manage her anxiety. She began to learn and practice relaxation techniques such as deep breathing exercises and visualization. Focusing on her breath, she brought her attention away from her fears and anxieties, grounding herself in the present. Visualization involved picturing a calming and peaceful scene or visualizing herself performing well in the exams. Over time, these techniques helped Sarah manage her anxiety effectively, improving her test scores and overall confidence. Sarah's story showcases the power of simple yet effective techniques in managing anxiety and improving one's quality of life. It's a testament to the fact that no matter how big or small the challenge, we can always take steps to manage our mental health better.

# PRACTICAL ADVICE AND TIPS

## Develop a Stress Management Toolbox

One of the essential strategies to combat stress and maintain mental well-being is creating a personal "Stress Management Toolbox." This toolbox consists of various activities and techniques to help you relax, find balance, and maintain a positive mindset. For some, physical exercises such as running, yoga, or even a brisk walk can be a great stress buster, releasing endorphins, the body's natural mood elevators. Others may find solace in expressive activities like journaling, which can provide an outlet for feelings and thoughts, aiding in self-reflection and understanding.

Practicing mindfulness, such as meditation or mindful breathing, can also be an effective tool for calming the mind and staying focused in the present moment, away from anxieties of the past or future anxieties. Mindfulness involves focusing on the present moment without judgment. This can help you to develop a greater awareness of your thoughts, feelings, and physical sensations, allowing you to better manage stress and anxiety. Try incorporating mindfulness exercises, such as deep breathing or meditation, into your daily routine.

Your stress management toolbox should be personal, filled with activities you enjoy and find beneficial in reducing stress and promoting mental well-being.

# Prioritize Self-Care

Another crucial aspect of maintaining mental well-being is prioritizing self-care. While the term *self-care* has become a popular buzzword, it's more than just a trend; it's an essential practice that involves taking care of your physical, emotional, and mental health. This could include scheduling regular daily breaks to engage in activities that bring you joy, rejuvenate your mind, and recharge your batteries. This could be as simple as reading a book, spending time in nature, playing a musical instrument, or connecting with friends. Self-care also includes maintaining a balanced diet, getting enough sleep, and staying physically active. By prioritizing self-care, you're acknowledging that your well-being matters and that you're worth the time and effort.

# Seek Professional Help When Needed

While self-help strategies can be highly beneficial in managing stress and maintaining mental well-being, there may be times when professional help is necessary. If you find yourself constantly struggling with high levels of stress, anxiety, or other mental health concerns that interfere with your daily life, don't hesitate to seek help from a mental health professional. This could involve talking to a psychologist, psychiatrist, or a trained counselor who can provide professional advice, therapeutic strategies, and in some cases, medication. It's important to remember that seeking help is not a sign of weakness but rather an act of courage and self-love. In fact, reaching out to professionals when needed is an integral part of a comprehensive mental health strategy. They can provide a safe space to express your thoughts and feelings, offer a new perspective, and provide you with the tools and techniques to manage your mental health effectively.

# WRITING PROMPTS AND REFLECTION QUESTIONS

* Reflect on situations that cause you stress or anxiety. What coping strategies have you used in the past, and how effective were they?

* How can you incorporate self-care into your daily routine to support your mental well-being?

# KEY TAKEAWAYS

**Identify and understand the sources of your stress and anxiety.**

The first step in managing stress and anxiety is identifying and understanding their sources. These can vary from person to person, including academic pressures, social challenges, or personal issues. Understanding your stress and anxiety triggers can help you develop effective coping strategies and improve your mental health.

**Develop a stress management toolbox with activities and techniques that work for you.**

Having a range of activities and techniques at your disposal can be incredibly useful in managing stress. This "toolbox" could include anything that helps you to relax and unwind, such as exercise, journaling, mindfulness, or listening to music. The key is to experiment and find out what works best for you.

**Prioritize self-care and make time for activities that bring you joy and relaxation.**

Self-care is an essential component of managing stress and maintaining mental well-being. This means taking regular breaks and making time for activities that bring joy, relaxation, and fulfillment. This could be spending time in nature, catching up with friends, reading a book, or even simply having a relaxing bath. Prioritizing self-care helps you to recharge and better cope with stress.

**Reach out for professional help when needed.**

There's no shame in seeking help if you're struggling with stress, anxiety, or other mental health concerns. Mental health professionals such as psychologists, psychiatrists, or counselors can provide valuable support and strategies to help you manage these challenges. Remember, asking for help is not a sign of weakness but rather a proactive step toward maintaining your mental health.

**Practice mindfulness to develop greater self-awareness and manage stress.**

Mindfulness involves being fully present and engaged in the current moment. By focusing on your feelings, thoughts, and sensations in the present moment, you can develop greater self-awareness, manage stress more effectively, and improve your mental well-being. This can be achieved through meditation, mindful breathing, or simply pausing and checking in with yourself during the day.

# INTERACTIVE ACTIVITIES AND EXERCISES

* Practice mindfulness meditation: Set aside five to ten minutes each day to practice mindfulness meditation, focusing on your breath and gently bringing your attention back whenever your mind wanders.

* Guided meditation: Find a quiet space and follow along with a guided meditation video or audio recording. Focus on your breath and gently bring your attention to the present moment whenever your mind wanders.

* Create a self-care plan: Design a self-care plan incorporating activities you enjoy and strategies for managing stress and commit to following it regularly.

# QUOTES TO INSPIRE AND MOTIVATE

"You don't have to control your thoughts. You just have to stop letting them control you."

—DAN MILLMAN

"It's not stress that kills us, it is our reaction to it."

—HANS SELYE

"Life is tough, my darling, but so are you."

—STEPHANIE BENNETT-HENRY

"You don't have to control your thoughts. You just have to stop letting them control you."

—DAN MILLMAN

## Focus on Role Models

**Emma Stone** epitomizes the importance of prioritizing mental health by being open about her experiences with anxiety and stress. Through her openness and advocacy, she has encouraged others to seek support and develop strategies for managing their mental well-being.

**Jazz Jennings:** The transgender teen and TV personality has faced her fair share of stress and anxiety, but she's taken proactive steps to manage her mental health and has used her platform to raise awareness about the mental health struggles faced by many in the transgender community.

**Hailee Steinfeld:** The actress and singer has often talked about the stress and pressure of being in the entertainment industry at a young age. She practices self-care and mindfulness techniques to manage her stress and has become an advocate for mental health.

A high school student, **Sarah** grappled with intense test anxiety that hampered her performance. She effectively managed her anxiety by learning and applying relaxation techniques such as deep breathing and visualization, improving her exam scores, and boosting her confidence.

# FINDING CALM IN THE STORM

There was a time when stress and anxiety seemed to have taken the driver's seat. It was during my final year of high school, a pivotal time fraught with academic pressures, college applications, and the impending transition to a new chapter in life. I felt the weight of expectations—from my teachers, my parents, and, most pressingly, myself.

I juggled AP classes, club leadership roles, part-time work, and deciding where to attend college. I began to experience sleepless nights, constant worry, and a feeling of overwhelming dread that seemed to follow me everywhere.

One day, my guidance counselor noticed my visible distress and asked me about it. I confessed my feelings of overwhelming stress and anxiety. I'll never forget her words that day, "Life is not a sprint; it's a marathon. You can't outrun stress, but you can learn to manage it."

Taking her advice, I took proactive steps toward managing my stress. I remembered how much I had enjoyed dancing and how it had helped me appreciate my body. So, I decided to rekindle my interest, this time to cope with stress.

Initially, switching off my spiraling thoughts during dance sessions felt almost impossible. But gradually, I learned to let the rhythm of the music guide me, allowing my body to move freely. Dancing became my outlet, my sanctuary where I could express my emotions without judgment.

In addition to dancing, I started practicing mindfulness meditation. Initially, I found it challenging to focus and quiet my mind. Still, with consistent practice, I began to experience moments of peace and tranquility. These quiet moments allowed me to observe my thoughts and feelings without getting swept away by them.

By carving out these spaces for myself, I began to gain control over my stress and anxiety. I could take a step back, breathe, and handle one thing at a time instead of getting overwhelmed by my responsibilities.

The dance classes and meditation didn't magically erase my stress and anxiety. Still, they provided me with tools to manage them. I was still navigating a challenging time but felt better equipped to handle it. It was like learning to dance in the rain instead of waiting for the storm to pass.

Looking back, this period of my life taught me invaluable lessons about managing stress and prioritizing mental well-being. Life will always bring challenges, but with the right tools and mindset, we can dance through the storm and find our calm within it.

# PRIORITIZING MENTAL WELL-BEING

In this comprehensive chapter, we have delved into the pivotal realm of managing stress, anxiety, and other mental health challenges often accompanying adolescence—a transformative period filled with a spectrum of emotions and experiences. As part of our exploration, we discussed various strategies, each aimed at helping you cope with these challenges and thrive amidst them.

We started the chapter by illuminating the importance of stress management and equipping you with a toolbox of practical activities and techniques tailored to your relaxation and relief. Integrating exercises, journaling, and mindfulness into your routine can cultivate an inner sanctuary of calm and resilience against the whirlwind of external pressures.

We then highlighted the importance of self-care, emphasizing its nonnegotiable role in preserving your mental well-being. From scheduling regular breaks and indulging in joy-sparking activities to ensuring a balanced diet and adequate sleep, self-care is the bedrock of your psychological and physical health.

Next, we addressed the vital role of professional help when dealing with heightened stress, anxiety, or other mental health concerns. We reassured you that seeking professional assistance is a courageous act of self-love and a vital aspect of a well-rounded mental health strategy.

We supplemented these strategies with real-life stories that bear testimony to the power of resilience and a proactive approach toward mental health. Our spotlight shone on role models like the acclaimed actress Emma Stone, who has used her platform to openly discuss her journey with anxiety, and Sarah, a high school student who successfully overcame test anxiety through relaxation techniques. These examples inspire and validate your experiences, showing you that you're not alone and that triumph over mental health challenges is possible.

As we wrap up this chapter, we encourage you to embrace these lessons, internalize the strategies, and, most importantly, remember that your mental well-being is worthy of care and attention. Your journey through adolescence may be filled with challenges but equipped with these tools and inspired by our role models, you can navigate this path with strength, balance, and a healthy mind. As you forge ahead, may you cultivate a deep sense of resilience and foster a compassionate relationship with your mind, for in prioritizing your mental health, you are setting the foundation for a fulfilling, joyful, and successful life.

# CHAPTER 7

## Set and Achieve Goals

In this chapter, we will get into one of your most powerful tools: setting and achieving goals. Whether you aim to ace your exams, become the star player in your soccer team, land the leading role in the school play, or work toward saving up for your first car, having clear, achievable goals is your game plan to turn dreams into reality. So, buckle up and get ready as we navigate the fun, sometimes tricky, but ultimately rewarding world of goal setting!

First off, we'll be exploring how to set realistic goals. We all dream big—and that's awesome—but understanding how to break down these dreams into manageable, achievable goals is the key. Trust me—there's nothing more satisfying than ticking off a goal from your list! We'll talk about how to set goals that are just the right size—not too easy that you breeze through them but not too difficult that they feel impossible.

Now, when we talk about achieving goals, we must consider time management. You've only got twenty-four hours a day, and juggling school, extracurricular activities, hanging out with friends, and personal downtime can be a lot! But don't worry; we've got your back. We will share some practical tips and strategies to help you manage your time more effectively, reduce stress, and ensure you have enough time to work toward your goals without missing out on the fun stuff.

Finally, what's the point of setting goals if you lose interest halfway? That's why we'll dive into understanding motivation and resilience. Keeping our spirits high and staying committed can sometimes be more challenging than setting goals. But with the right mindset and some handy tips, you'll be more than ready to stay focused, overcome obstacles, and power through to achieve your goals.

This chapter does not just discuss ticking boxes off a list. We're delving into a significant life skill that will empower you not just in your teenage years but throughout your life. Goal setting isn't just for school or career aspirations; it's for everything you want to achieve. By mastering these skills now, you're setting yourself up for a great future where you can effectively chase your dreams and make them a reality. So, let's start this exciting journey to becoming the best goal setting, goal-crushing version of you!

# REAL-LIFE STORIES

## The Journey of Simone Biles

### SETTING THE BAR HIGH, AGAIN AND AGAIN

Simone Biles, an icon in gymnastics, is a shining example of how determination, hard work, and a clear vision can pave the way to unparalleled success. Born in 1997 in Columbus, Ohio, Simone's early life was marked by struggles. Born to a drug-addicted mother, she shuffled between foster homes until her grandparents adopted her at age six. Despite her challenges, Simone found a sanctuary in gymnastics, her passion and natural talent shining through from the moment she first tried out the sport.

However, the path to success had its challenges. Simone had to grapple with a demanding training schedule, grueling physical and mental challenges, and the public scrutiny that comes with being an athlete in the public eye. Despite the obstacles, Simone remained unwavering in her pursuit of her goals. She trained tirelessly, often pushing through injuries and setbacks, proving that one could rise to the top with resilience and hard work.

Her efforts paid off. Today, Simone Biles is the most decorated gymnast in World Championship history. Her talent and dedication have seen her shatter numerous records, claiming an impressive array of medals and earning her a place among the greatest gymnasts the world has ever seen. But what is most inspiring about Simone's story is her unyielding determination and resilience. Despite the adversities she faced in her personal life and professional career, she never wavered from her goal of reaching the pinnacle of her sport.

Simone's journey is a testament to what can be achieved when you set clear goals and pursue them with unwavering determination and grit.

# *Mikaila Ulmer*
## A YOUNG ENTREPRENEUR WITH A MISSION

Mikaila Ulmer's story is one of youthful ambition, dedication, and environmental advocacy. At just four years old, Mikaila started what would become a thriving lemonade business, Me & the Bees Lemonade, spurred by a family recipe and a passion for saving honeybees. While many children her age focused on play and school, Mikaila was setting and achieving business goals.

After a bee sting led her to learn more about bees' crucial role in our ecosystem and the threats they face, Mikaila was inspired to help. She decided to create a product that would educate about the bees' importance and contribute to their preservation. Her grandmother's flaxseed lemonade recipe was the perfect solution.

Despite her young age, Mikaila displayed exceptional dedication and business acumen. She successfully pitched her business on the popular TV show *Shark Tank*, securing an investment that boosted her company's growth. Today, Me & the Bees Lemonade is sold in stores across the US, and a portion of the profits goes to organizations fighting to save honeybees.

Mikaila's journey is an inspiring example of setting ambitious goals and achieving them. She shows that age is no barrier to entrepreneurship or environmental activism and that great things can be achieved with dedication, creativity, and a strong sense of purpose.

# Emma González

## A VOICE FOR CHANGE

Emma González's journey is a powerful story of resilience, advocacy, and the impact of youth voices in shaping societal change. As a survivor of the 2018 Marjory Stoneman Douglas High School shooting, Emma transformed a devastating experience into a powerful campaign for gun control.

Emma and other survivors cofounded the Never Again MSD, a student-led political action committee advocating for gun control and against gun violence. The group organized the March For Our Lives event, one of the largest protests in American history, drawing hundreds of thousands of participants.

Through impassioned speeches and public appearances, Emma helped thrust the issue of gun control back into the national spotlight. Her courage, tenacity, and commitment to her cause have made her a potent symbol of youth activism and an inspiration for other young people.

Emma González's story is a testament to the power of young people in driving change. She demonstrates that young people can effect significant societal change with a clear goal, unwavering determination, and the courage to speak up.

# *Tavi Gevinson*

## SHAPING CONVERSATIONS,
## ONE POST AT A TIME

Tavi Gevinson's story is one of youthful creativity, ambition, and the power of the internet in fostering discussions and building communities. As a teenager, Tavi leveraged her love for fashion and writing to create a blog, *Style Rookie*. However, her next venture, *Rookie* magazine, truly demonstrated her ability to set and achieve ambitious goals.

At just fifteen, Tavi identified a gap in the market for a space where teenage girls could discuss popular culture and feminism. She envisioned a platform to empower young women, providing a space for intelligent discourse, creative expression, and community-building.

*Rookie* launched in 2011 and was precisely that. The online publication quickly gained a dedicated readership and critical acclaim, with content ranging from personal essays and advice columns to interviews, artwork, and playlists.

Tavi's journey is a testament to the power of setting and achieving goals. By identifying and working to fill a need, she created a space that empowered young women, championed their voices, and facilitated thoughtful discussions. Tavi Gevinson shows us that age is no barrier to creating something meaningful, impactful, and lasting.

These journeys underscore the power of setting clear goals and pursuing them with unwavering determination. The stories above testify to the heights one can achieve with grit, passion, and a clear vision. In the face of adversity, these role models remained resolute, proving that one's circumstances don't define them—it's the will to rise above these challenges that truly counts.

# PRACTICAL ADVICE AND TIPS

## *Implement* SMART *Goals*

An effective goal-setting strategy involves making them SMART—Specific, Measurable, Achievable, Relevant, and Time-bound. This approach ensures your ambitions are clear and realistic and offer a well-defined path to success. Specificity eliminates vagueness, making your goal more tangible. Measurability allows for tracking progress and identifying when the goal has been reached. Ensuring your goal is achievable protects your motivation by not setting yourself up for an impossible task. Relevance ensures your goal aligns with your broader ambitions, values, and immediate needs. Finally, time-bound means each goal has a deadline, creating a sense of urgency and momentum.

Here's an example of setting a SMART goal. Let's say your passion is writing, and you want to improve your storytelling skills. You can set a SMART goal like this:

* Specific: "I want to write a short story of at least one thousand words."

* Measurable: "I will track my progress by keeping a word count journal and aiming to write at least two hundred words daily."

* Achievable: "Considering my current writing abilities and available time, I can complete the short story within one month."

* Relevant: "Improving my storytelling skills will contribute to my goal of becoming a better writer and pursuing creative writing in the future."

* Time-bound: "I will complete the short story by the end of next month."

By setting a SMART goal like this, you have a clear objective and a plan to work toward it. You can break down the task into smaller daily or weekly targets, monitor your progress, and adjust as needed. This approach provides structure, motivation, and a sense of accomplishment as you move closer to achieving your goal.

## Break Down Larger Goals into Smaller Tasks

Big goals can sometimes be intimidating, which may hinder your progress. The solution is to divide them into smaller, manageable tasks. Each task acts as a stepping stone toward the larger goal, making the journey feel less daunting. The satisfaction of completing these tasks not only fuels motivation but also generates a sense of accomplishment and progress. Remember, every significant achievement is but a series of small victories.

## Establish a Routine

Consistency is critical to achieving any goal. Establishing a daily or weekly routine can be crucial in maintaining your progress. It's not just about allocating dedicated time to work on your goals; it's about making goal progression an integral part of your life. By integrating time for your goals into your routine, you're creating a sustainable habit, reducing the reliance on fleeting motivation. A routine can provide a sense of order and control over your time and energy, which can help you stay focused, maintain momentum, and ultimately accelerate your journey toward your goals.

## Practice Consistency and Patience

Achieving any important goal requires consistency and patience. It's essential to understand that progress might not always be linear. There might be setbacks and slow periods; however, what matters is to keep moving forward. The steady, continued effort leads to substantial change over time. Remember, Rome wasn't built in a day.

## Maintain a Positive Attitude

Your mindset plays a significant role in approaching and achieving your goals. Maintaining a positive attitude helps you better cope with challenges, bounce back from failures, and stay focused on your objectives. Even when things get tough, a positive mindset can help you find the silver lining and provide the mental strength to push forward.

## *Seek Support When Needed*

Remember, you don't have to do it all alone. Seeking help or guidance when you need it is not a sign of weakness but a strength. Whether it's a mentor, a supportive friend, or a professional, having a support network can provide valuable feedback, encouragement, and different perspectives that can assist you in reaching your goals.

Remember, these strategies are not one-size-fits-all. You should tweak them or use different combinations depending on your specific goals and circumstances. The key is to stay flexible, adapt when needed, and keep your eyes on the prize.

# WRITING PROMPTS AND REFLECTION QUESTIONS

* Reflect on a goal you have achieved in the past. What strategies did you use to reach this goal, and what did you learn from the experience?

* Consider a current goal you have set for yourself. How can you apply the SMART criteria to ensure this goal is clear, realistic, and trackable?

* What obstacles might you face as you work toward your goals, and how can you plan to overcome them?

# KEY TAKEAWAYS

**Set SMART goals to ensure they are clear, realistic, and trackable.**

SMART is an acronym for Specific, Measurable, Achievable, Relevant, and Time-bound. This strategy ensures your goals are clear and reachable. When setting your goals, make sure they are specific and well-defined, measurable so you can track your progress, achievable to keep you motivated, relevant to your broader life goals, and time-bound to provide a sense of urgency and keep you on track.

**Break down larger goals into smaller, manageable tasks.**

Achieving an important goal can sometimes seem overwhelming. One way to make this process easier and more manageable is to break your larger goal into smaller tasks or sub-goals. This makes it easier to focus on the immediate steps you need to take. It can also provide a sense of accomplishment as you tick off each task, maintaining your motivation.

**Develop a plan of action and establish a timeline for achieving your goals.**

Creating an action plan is an essential step toward achieving your goals. An action plan helps to organize your tasks, assign responsibilities (if applicable), and set a timeline for completion.

A clear plan and timeline guide you, keeping you focused and motivated as you work toward your goal.

**Maintain motivation and resilience.**

When working toward a goal, staying motivated and resilient is essential. There will likely be obstacles and setbacks, but don't let these discourage you. Instead, use them as learning experiences and adjust your action plan if necessary. Remember why your goal is essential, celebrate your progress, and maintain a positive mindset to keep your motivation high.

# INTERACTIVE ACTIVITIES AND EXERCISES

*   Goal-setting worksheet: Create a worksheet that guides you through setting SMART goals, breaking them down into smaller tasks, and developing a plan of action.

*   Vision board: Create a visual representation of your goals using images, quotes, and other inspiring elements. Display your vision board in a prominent place as a daily reminder of your aspirations.

# QUOTES TO INSPIRE AND MOTIVATE

"Success is the sum of small efforts, repeated day in and day out."
—ROBERT COLLIER

"The only limit to the height of your achievements is the reach of your dreams and your willingness to work for them."

—MICHELLE OBAMA

## Focus on Role Models

**Simone Biles:** As a world-class gymnast, Simone Biles exemplifies the power of setting and achieving goals. Her unwavering dedication and determination have propelled her to the pinnacle of her sport, inspiring countless young athletes to pursue their dreams.

**Mikaila Ulmer:** As a young entrepreneur and advocate for environmental conservation, Mikaila Ulmer demonstrates the power of setting and achieving goals. Her passion for making a positive impact has driven her business success and inspired others to follow in her footsteps.

**Emma González:** Emma set a goal to advocate for gun control following the tragic shooting at her high school in Parkland, Florida. She has since cofounded the Never Again MSD group and organized the March for Our Lives.

**Tavi Gevinson:** Tavi set a goal to create a platform for teenage girls to discuss popular culture and feminism, and she achieved this by founding *Rookie* magazine when she was just fifteen.

# A RACE AGAINST TIME

Growing up, I was never what you would call an "athletic" kid, and I was more at home in a library than on a sports field. However, I dealt with a growing concern about my fitness level during college. I was frequently short of breath, and my energy levels were consistently low. That's when I decided I needed to make a change for the better and set a SMART goal to do just that.

My specific goal was to run a half-marathon. It was measurable—a total of 13.1 miles, and I thought it achievable with the proper training and consistency, despite my lack of prior running experience. This was relevant because it directly impacted my health and wellness. The time-bound aspect was the local annual half-marathon event date, which gave me ten months to prepare.

To make my goal a reality, I researched beginner running plans and slowly introduced jogging into my routine. Initially, I could only run for a few minutes before feeling winded.

But I persisted, gradually increasing my running intervals each week.

Tracking my progress was instrumental in keeping me motivated. Each extra minute I could run, or every additional mile I covered, was a victory. These miles were tangible signs that I was getting stronger and closer to my goal.

Balancing school, a part-time job, and my running regimen was challenging. There were moments when I questioned my ability to reach my goal. It seemed easier to give up, but I held onto my vision. I envisioned myself crossing the finish line, and the thought filled me with determination.

When the day of the half-marathon finally arrived, I was a bundle of nerves. As I started running, though, I found my rhythm. Each mile marker I passed filled me with a sense of achievement. When I crossed the finish line, I felt pride and fulfillment. It wasn't just the physical accomplishment of running 13.1 miles but the realization that I had taken control of my health and pushed my boundaries.

In retrospect, setting a SMART goal to run a half-marathon was one of my best decisions as a teenager. It improved my fitness and instilled in me the confidence and resilience to face challenges head-on. The lessons I learned from this experience continue to influence my goal-setting approach in all aspects of my life.

# HARNESSING THE POWER
# OF GOAL SETTING

This chapter has unearthed the pivotal role of setting, working toward, and achieving goals when building robust confidence and designing a genuinely fulfilling and rewarding life. We've unraveled the mystery of SMART goals—Specific, Measurable, Achievable, Relevant, and Time-bound—and how these clear, well-defined objectives can ignite your motivation and propel you toward your aspirations.

In addition, we've demystified the process of breaking complex goals into smaller, manageable tasks, making them less intimidating and more accessible. We've underlined the importance of having a consistent action plan and nurturing a routine that accommodates dedicated time for pursuing these objectives. This approach doesn't only ensure your journey is structured and organized. Still, it guarantees steady and sustainable progress, further reinforcing your confidence.

In our quest to comprehend the power of goal setting, we've been inspired by luminaries like Simone Biles and Mikaila Ulmer, titans in their fields. These role models are living testimonials of what persistence, ambition, and a clear vision can accomplish. They've proven time and time again that fortified by dedication, determination, and a well-thought-out plan, one can surmount hurdles and make dreams come alive.

As we turn the page and prepare for the upcoming chapters, let's carry forward the valuable lessons from this section. It's your turn to employ these strategies and tips to set and work tirelessly toward your unique goals. Doing so will supercharge your confidence and lay a solid groundwork for imminent success and continued personal growth. Remember, your path is yours to create, and your dreams are yours to realize. Onward!

**CHAPTER 8**

# Explore Interests and Passions

We're about to embark on an exciting journey in Chapter 8—exploring your unique interests and passions. The world is brimming with endless possibilities and opportunities, and it's important to discover what truly captures your curiosity and enthusiasm.

Finding and pursuing your passions can significantly improve self-confidence and personal development. It's about more than having a hobby; it's about understanding who you are, what you love, and how those passions shape your identity.

In this chapter, we'll delve into the significance of self-discovery, the value of hobbies, the impact of engaging in extracurricular activities, and how all these aspects facilitate personal growth.

Moreover, we'll draw motivation from inspiring individuals such as Greta Thunberg and JoJo Siwa. Thunberg, a devoted environmental activist, ignited a global movement from her passion for protecting the planet. Siwa, on the other hand, transformed her love for dance and music into a successful career that resonates with millions of young people worldwide.

Their stories exemplify the immense power and potential that lie in pursuing our interests. Ready to uncover your passions and see where they might lead? Let's dive in.

# REAL-LIFE STORIES

## Greta Thunberg

### DISCOVERING A CAUSE AND IGNITING A GLOBAL MOVEMENT

Hailing from Stockholm, Sweden, Greta Thunberg's journey into climate activism is a tale of tremendous determination and passion that began with a solitary act. At the tender age of fifteen, she was deeply disturbed by the world's apparent indifference to the looming environmental crisis. She decided she could no longer stand by and do nothing. Motivated by a profound sense of duty to her generation and future ones, she took the bold step of skipping school to protest outside the Swedish Parliament. This was not an act of rebellion but a plea for action.

Her steadfast resolve and singular focus on demanding adequate action against climate change caught the world's attention. Armed with a homemade sign that read "School strike for the climate" and facts backed by scientific research, she engaged with curious passersby, articulating the urgent need for immediate action. Social media helped amplify her message, and before long, Greta Thunberg, the quiet teenager from Sweden, became the face of a global youth-led movement for climate justice.

The Fridays for Future movement, as it came to be known, saw students from across the world leave their classrooms and take to the streets, inspired by Greta's unyielding courage and resolve. What began as a solitary protest outside her local parliament rapidly evolved into an international movement, galvanizing millions of young people to champion the cause of climate justice. Greta Thunberg was not just a protester but a catalyst, sparking a global awakening to the urgency of the climate crisis.

Greta's fierce dedication stems from her deep passion for the environment, a passion she has managed to channel into a cause larger than herself. Her story is one of hope, resilience, and belief in the power of change, even if it begins with a single individual. She inspires all, showing us the ripple effect that one person, no matter how young, can create when their passion is directed toward a cause they truly care about.

Greta's journey is not just a testament to her drive and determination; it also underscores the power and potential that arise from nurturing one's interests and utilizing them to effect change in the world. This is the lesson of Greta Thunberg: when passion and perseverance align with a purpose, the impact can echo around the world, urging us all to sit up, listen, and take action.

# JoJo Siwa

## A VIBRANT JOURNEY FROM DANCE
## TO DIVERSE CREATIVE PURSUITS

JoJo Siwa, born Joelle Joanie Siwa, is a true shining star whose vibrant personality is as infectious as her colorful oversized bows. Hailing from Omaha, Nebraska, JoJo's journey into the limelight started at a young age when she first appeared on the reality show *Abby's Ultimate Dance Competition*. Despite being the youngest contestant, her tenacity and raw talent soon caught the attention of many.

After the competition, JoJo continued to hone her skills and pursued her passion for dance and performance, later becoming a breakout star on the hit reality show *Dance Moms*. But dancing was just one facet of JoJo's multifaceted talent. Her infectious energy and vibrant personality also lent themselves to music, leading her to a successful career as a pop singer, with hits like "Boomerang" and "Kid in a Candy Store."

More than just an entertainer, JoJo has become a role model for millions of young fans worldwide. Her flamboyant style, characterized by bright colors and signature hair bows, symbolizes self-expression and positivity. She encourages her fans, known as Siwanatorz, to be confident, embrace their individuality, and have fun.

JoJo, who's queer, recently came out as pansexual and has become a big name in the young gay community. Her identity? It's a huge part of what she's about. As I'm writing this, her Pride collection is the first thing you see on her website.

# Brittany Wenger

## HARNESSING TECHNOLOGY
## FOR A GREATER CAUSE

Brittany Wenger's journey merges passion with purpose, science with service. A bright mind from Sarasota, Florida, Brittany's interest in science was sparked at a young age when her cousin was diagnosed with breast cancer. Determined to make a difference, she focused on harnessing artificial intelligence's power to improve breast cancer diagnostics.

At just seventeen years old, Brittany developed a groundbreaking artificial intelligence program capable of accurately diagnosing breast cancer. Her program, Cloud4Cancer, uses a complex artificial neural network to analyze patterns and detect malignancies in breast masses. Brittany's project won the Grand Prize at the Google Science Fair 2012. It opened new avenues in medical diagnostics and treatment.

Brittany's story is a testament to the transformative power of technology when placed in the hands of someone fueled by passion and determination. It showcases the potential within each of us to leverage our interests and skills to create positive change in the world.

# Autumn Peltier

## A VOICE FOR THE WATERS

Autumn Peltier, an Anishinaabe teenager from the Wikwemikong First Nation in Canada, is a passionate advocate for water conservation. Recognizing the sacredness of water in her culture and its critical role in sustaining life, Autumn has dedicated herself to protecting water resources.

Inspired by her great aunt, Josephine Mandamin, a prominent water activist, Autumn began speaking out about water conservation and indigenous water rights at a young age. Her advocacy has taken her to stages worldwide, including the United Nations, where she has eloquently spoken about the need for action to protect the world's water.

Autumn's journey is an inspiring example of how passion and a deep sense of responsibility can drive significant change. Despite her youth, she has become a powerful voice for water conservation, inspiring individuals and communities to respect and protect this vital resource.

The remarkable journeys of Greta Thunberg, JoJo Siwa, Brittany Wenger, and Autumn Peltier illustrate the incredible potential of harnessing personal passions for a broader purpose. In her unique way, each has inspired, influenced, and made significant strides in climate justice, self-expression, technological innovation, and environmental conservation. Their stories serve as potent reminders that age or circumstance need not limit the capacity to explore interests and make a meaningful impact. They embody the transformative power of passion, determination, and purpose, reminding us all that it's never too early to start making a difference in the world.

# PRACTICAL ADVICE AND TIPS

## Try New Activities

The first step toward discovering your passions is experimenting and exploring various activities. Try joining various clubs, attending diverse workshops, participating in local events, or volunteering in your community. Exposing yourself to different experiences broadens your horizons and increases your chances of finding something that ignites your enthusiasm.

## Reflect on Your Experiences

After dipping your toes into different activities, take a moment to reflect on your experiences. Consider what you enjoyed most and why. Did a particular activity make your heart race with excitement? Or did you lose track of time because you were so engrossed in a task? Reflecting on these experiences can provide valuable insights into your passions. It can guide you toward areas you wish to delve into more deeply.

## Connect with Like-Minded Individuals

In exploring your interests, seek out groups, clubs, or online communities that align with your passions. These environments are rich in inspiration, motivation, and support and can provide valuable opportunities for collaboration. Engaging with like-minded individuals can help sustain your interest and passion, providing a sense of belonging and encouragement.

## Set Goals Related to Your Interests

Upon identifying your passions, aim to set specific, measurable, achievable, relevant, and time-bound (SMART) goals related to your interests. Goals provide direction, helping to keep your passion alive and thriving. They also facilitate continuous growth and development in your areas of interest.

## Be Open to Change

Lastly, be open to change. Your interests and passions may evolve as you continue to grow and develop. This change isn't something to fear but to welcome. Remaining flexible and open to new experiences allows you to continually discover and redefine your passions. By embracing change, you allow your journey of self-discovery and personal growth to flourish unbounded.

# WRITING PROMPTS AND REFLECTION QUESTIONS

* List three activities or hobbies you would like to try. What draws you to these activities?

* Think about a time when you felt truly passionate about something. What was it, and what about it made you feel so passionate?

* How can you incorporate your passions into your daily life? How can doing so benefit your well-being and confidence?

* What obstacles or fears might be holding you back from pursuing your interests? How can you overcome them?

# KEY TAKEAWAYS

**Discovering your passions and interests can help you develop a well-rounded sense of self.**

Discovering your passions and interests is essential in personal growth and developing a well-rounded sense of self. Engaging with what truly excites and drives you brings joy and fulfillment and shapes your character, values, and perspectives.

**Trying new activities and reflecting on your experiences can help you identify your passions.**

Exploring new activities, hobbies, and experiences is a fantastic way to uncover potential passions. It's okay if you don't immediately know your passions; discovering them is a journey. After trying something new, reflect on your experiences. Did you feel energized, engaged, and eager to do it again? If so, you might have found a new passion.

**Connecting with like-minded individuals can provide motivation and support as you pursue your interests.**

Finding a community of like-minded individuals who share your passions and interests can be incredibly rewarding. This connection can offer support, motivation, and inspiration, enhancing your experiences and learning. Such communities can be found in clubs, online forums, or social media groups.

**Setting goals related to your passions can help you stay focused and motivated.**

Once you've discovered your passions, setting goals related to them can help you stay focused and motivated. These goals provide a clear direction to channel your energy and keep you engaged in your passion. Remember to set SMART goals to ensure they are clear, achievable, and meaningful.

**Embrace change and remain open to exploring new hobbies and activities.**

Remembering that our passions and interests can evolve is important. Embrace change and remain open to trying new things. Exploring different hobbies and activities can lead to personal growth, new skills, and unexpected passions. Stay curious, open-minded, and ready to explore—you never know where your next passion might come from.

# INTERACTIVE ACTIVITIES AND EXERCISES

* **Create a Passion Map:** Draw a mind map or create a collage representing your passions, interests, and goals. Use images, words, or phrases that resonate with you.

* **Thirty-Day Passion Challenge:** Choose a new hobby or activity to explore for the next thirty days. Dedicate at least fifteen minutes per day to this new interest. At the end of the thirty days, reflect on your experience and decide if it's something you'd like to continue pursuing.

* **Passion Journal:** Start a journal dedicated to your passions and interests. Use it to document your experiences, reflect on your feelings, and track your progress in developing your skills and knowledge.

* **Create a vision board:** Develop a vision board that represents your passions, goals, and aspirations. Include images, quotes, or phrases that inspire you. Display your vision board in a prominent place to remind you of your passions and encourage you to pursue them.

# QUOTES TO INSPIRE
# AND MOTIVATE

"Don't ask yourself what the world needs. Ask yourself what makes you come alive, and go do that, because what the world needs is people who have come alive."

## —HOWARD THURMAN

"There is no passion to be found playing small—in settling for a life that is less than the one you are capable of living."

## —NELSON MANDELA

"Your work is going to fill a large part of your life, and the only way to be truly satisfied is to do what you believe is great work. And the only way to do great work is to love what you do."

## —STEVE JOBS

"You can't connect the dots looking forward; you can only connect them looking backward. So you have to trust that the dots will somehow connect in your future. You have to trust in something—your gut, destiny, life, karma, whatever. This approach has never let me down, and it has made all the difference in my life."

## —STEVE JOBS

## Focus on Role Models

**Greta Thunberg**'s passion for climate change activism demonstrates the importance of exploring interests and taking action to make a difference. Her dedication and determination inspired millions of young people to join her in advocating for a better future.

**JoJo Siwa**'s career as a singer, dancer, and social media star encourages young girls to explore their interests and passions. She has inspired countless fans to do the same by expressing her individuality through creativity and self-expression.

**Brittany Wenger:** At seventeen, Brittany won the Google Science Fair for developing a cloud-based AI model to improve breast cancer diagnosis, demonstrating her passion for computer science and healthcare.

**Autumn Peltier:** Autumn is an indigenous clean water activist who began her advocacy work at eight and has since spoken at the United Nations, demonstrating her commitment to environmental activism.

# UNVEILING THE MYSTERIES
# OF HAITIAN MYTHOLOGY

Growing up in a Haitian household, I was surrounded by vibrant stories of *loas* (spirits), legendary heroes, and mysterious creatures deeply rooted in our cultural heritage. Yet, it was only in my teenage years that I began to understand the richness and depth of Haitian mythology.

I was fourteen when I stumbled upon a dusty, old book titled *Legends of Haiti* in the library. Out of curiosity, I started leafing through the pages. Before I knew it, I was engrossed in the tales of spirits like Papa Legba, the gatekeeper of the spirit world, and Grann Brijit, the queen of the cemetery.

The more I read, the more I became fascinated by these stories integral to my heritage. I realized that these myths and legends were more than just tales; they were a window into the soul of my people, providing insight into our beliefs, values, and history.

Eager to delve deeper, I attended cultural workshops the local Haitian community center organized. There, I learned about the Vodou religion, its rituals, symbolism, and the role these deities played in the daily lives of Haitians. This gave me an even greater appreciation for the richness and depth of my culture.

Moreover, the stories I encountered inspired me creatively. I began incorporating elements of Haitian mythology into my writing and artwork, infusing them with the vibrant energy and spirit of these age-old tales. My school projects on Haitian culture and mythology were well received, and my peers became more interested in learning about our diverse cultural backgrounds.

Exploring Haitian mythology did more than satisfy my curiosity; it sparked a passion that has stayed with me. It deepened my connection to my roots and gave me profound pride in my heritage. It led me to appreciate the power of storytelling and its ability to preserve culture, impart wisdom, and foster a sense of community.

Ignited by a dusty old book, this journey significantly shaped my identity and appreciation for cultural diversity. It has since then guided my personal and academic choices, leading me to major in anthropology in college, focusing on Caribbean cultures. My passion for Haitian mythology continues to grow, reminding me that our stories, like the *loas*, are ever-present, guiding us through life's journey.

# UNLEASHING YOUR PASSIONS

In this enriching chapter, we've taken a deep dive into the world of personal interests and passions, highlighting their pivotal role in developing a well-rounded and confident self-identity. We've learned that embracing your passions is about personal enjoyment and fostering personal growth, self-confidence, and impactful influence in the world around you.

The remarkable journeys of our role models, Greta Thunberg and JoJo Siwa, have shed light on the power of passion. They've shown us how deeply held interests can propel us to heights we may have never imagined, and how our individual voices can reverberate around the globe, inspiring change and making a difference.

Throughout this chapter, we've provided practical advice and actionable tips to guide you on your journey of self-discovery. You can uncover and nurture your unique interests by actively trying out new activities, reflecting thoughtfully on your experiences, creating connections with those with similar interests, and setting achievable goals related to your passions.

But let's not forget, life is a journey full of twists and turns. As you continue to grow and learn, your interests and passions may evolve and transform like you. It's essential to remain open to this change, embrace the flux, and see it as an exciting part of your self-discovery. Your interests and passions are like a compass, guiding your growth path and imbuing your life with excitement, meaning, and personal fulfillment. So, keep exploring, keep growing, and let your passions illuminate your path.

# CHAPTER 9

## *Prepare for Your Future*

This stage in your life as a teenager is not just about traversing through high school years; it's a pivotal moment that significantly shapes your future. The decisions you make, the goals you set, and the skills you acquire during these formative years can lay the foundation for the chapters ahead. The preparation begins now, whether it's higher education, your first job, or other adult responsibilities.

This chapter will equip you with essential guidance and practical advice to serve as your compass in this exciting journey toward your future. We will delve into crucial topics such as college preparation and its various aspects—from choosing the right course to the application process. We'll touch on career planning, an integral part of which is understanding your passions and strengths and aligning them with potential career paths. We'll also discuss the art of decision-making, a life skill that grows more critical as you enter adulthood.

However, preparing for the future is about more than just the academic and professional side of things. It's also about developing life skills to help you navigate the various situations and challenges you will encounter. This includes skills like effective communication, time management, problem-solving, and resilience.

To bring these concepts to life, we'll also delve into the inspiring stories of young women who have navigated their unique paths to success. Malia and Sasha Obama, the former First Daughters of the United States, have each carved out their journeys under the global spotlight, growing into accomplished young women while managing the pressures of their unique position. Similarly, Greta Thunberg, the Swedish environmental activist, turned her passion into a global movement while handling her educational pursuits and personal growth.

Despite their unique circumstances, these young women have become role models for young women worldwide, exemplifying that the choices and preparation during your teenage years can indeed shape the future in profound and fulfilling ways. Let their stories and the information and advice in this chapter guide you as you prepare for your exciting future.

# REAL-LIFE STORIES

## Malia Obama
### EXPLORING PASSIONS THROUGH PRACTICAL EXPOSURE

As the elder daughter of the forty-fourth president of the United States, Barack Obama, Malia Obama's life has been anything but ordinary. She was born and raised in the public eye, her adolescence unfolding on a global stage. Yet she managed to maintain a sense of normalcy and prioritize her growth and development. Despite the inevitable pressure and expectations, Malia's journey has been marked by a quiet determination to carve her own path and pursue her passions.

After graduating high school, Malia made a decision that reflected her keen sense of self-awareness and desire for growth: she chose to take a gap year. This was a unique choice, particularly for those in the public eye. Still, Malia saw it as an opportunity for practical exposure and self-exploration, away from the pressures of academia.

During this gap year, she interned in the film industry, immersing herself in a field she had long been passionate about. From script reading and pitching to assisting on sets, she spent her time understanding the industry's intricacies and learning about the behind-the-scenes work that goes into creating movies and TV shows.

This real-world experience allowed Malia to explore her creative interests more profoundly. It offered her invaluable insights into the practical aspects of filmmaking. It served as an extension of her academic pursuits and a catalyst to guide her future educational choices.

After her gap year, Malia enrolled at Harvard University. Going into her college education with practical industry experience, she was better equipped to make informed decisions about her studies and future career. Malia's journey, marked by her intentionality and the courage to follow her passions, inspires all young people preparing to navigate their futures. Her story reminds us that preparing for the future is not just about meeting expectations or following established paths but about exploring, understanding, and pursuing our passions.

# Sasha Obama

## CRAFTING HER UNIQUE PATH
## IN HIGHER EDUCATION

Sasha Obama, the younger of the Obama siblings, has gracefully navigated the challenges of growing up in the public eye. Like her elder sister, Malia, Sasha's youth was marked by extraordinary experiences—from meeting world leaders to residing in the White House. Yet, despite the unique circumstances of her upbringing, Sasha has remained grounded, developing into a strong, independent young woman with a clear sense of identity.

On graduating high school, Sasha faced a decision familiar to many her age—where to pursue higher education. It was a choice that would influence her academic future and shape her personal growth and professional development. As she weighed her options, Sasha was clear about one thing: she wished to carve out a path distinct from those her family followed.

Ultimately, Sasha decided to attend the University of Michigan, a public research university renowned for its commitment to social change and academic excellence. Unlike her sister, who chose the Ivy League experience at Harvard, Sasha opted for a different educational path. This decision reflected her interests and values, underscoring her desire to shape her journey. The University of Michigan's ethos of community engagement and social activism resonated with Sasha, aligning with her aspirations and the values she had grown up with.

Choosing a college may seem routine for many, but it was a defining moment for Sasha. It was an opportunity to step out of her family's shadows and forge her identity. Sasha's choice exemplifies the importance of aligning decisions with personal preferences and goals rather than conforming to external expectations or predetermined paths.

Her decision-making process reminds young individuals everywhere that preparing for the future involves making choices that reflect our unique aspirations and values. Sasha's story highlights the importance of authenticity in shaping our journeys, inspiring young people to carve out their paths and remain true to themselves.

## *Amika George*

## THE POWER OF YOUTH ACTIVISM

Amika George, a British activist from the United Kingdom, has emerged as a prominent voice for menstrual equity, demonstrating the immense potential of youth activism. Growing up in a world where period poverty—the lack of access to sanitary products due to financial constraints—was a rarely discussed issue, Amika felt a pressing need to address this significant but overlooked problem.

While still in high school, Amika began the #FreePeriods campaign, advocating for free menstrual products for those in need. The campaign started as a simple petition but quickly became a widespread movement, culminating in a peaceful protest outside Downing Street. Amika's tireless advocacy paid off when the UK government committed to funding free sanitary products in all English schools and colleges, marking a significant victory for menstrual equity.

Amika's story is a shining example of how an individual's passion, determination, and perseverance can lead to systemic change. It also underscores the importance of preparing for the future—not just on a personal level but on a societal level too. Through her activism, Amika has not only paved the way for her future but has also influenced the future of countless individuals affected by period poverty.

Amika George has shown the world that age is no barrier to making a significant impact. She represents the power of youth, the potential for change, and the importance of standing up for what you believe in. As she continues her journey, Amika inspires young people everywhere to be catalysts for change, demonstrating that our actions can shape a more equitable and inclusive future.

# Naomi Osaka
## MASTERING THE GAME ON AND OFF THE COURT

Japanese professional tennis player Naomi Osaka has made her mark both on and off the court, demonstrating an extraordinary blend of talent, resilience, and social consciousness. Bursting onto the international tennis scene at a young age, Naomi's powerful game and unwavering determination have catapulted her to the pinnacle of her sport. However, her maturity, grace, and commitment to social issues off the court truly set her apart.

Naomi's rise to prominence in tennis is a testament to her diligent preparation for the future. Years of rigorous training, strategic planning, and mental conditioning have helped her amass many accolades, including multiple Grand Slam titles.

Her performances highlight the significance of setting and pursuing ambitious goals, reinforcing the value of preparation, perseverance, and self-belief.

However, Naomi's influence extends far beyond the tennis court. She has utilized her platform to raise awareness of social and racial injustice, notably wearing masks emblazoned with the names of Black individuals who lost their lives due to police violence. Her actions highlight the importance of social consciousness and the potential of individuals to affect change, even as they pursue personal ambitions.

Balancing the demands of a high-pressure sporting career with a commitment to social activism is no easy task, but Naomi manages it with aplomb. She is unafraid to prioritize her mental health, demonstrating a maturity and self-awareness that belies her years. Her decision to withdraw from prestigious tournaments to protect her mental well-being underscores the importance of self-care in preparing for a sustainable and fulfilling future.

Naomi Osaka's journey so far has been one of unwavering commitment to her sport, social causes, and self-care. She exemplifies the multifaceted nature of preparation for the future, embodying the blend of personal growth, professional success, and social responsibility that defines modern-day success. Through her actions, Naomi inspires young people to prepare for their futures by pursuing their passions, standing up for their beliefs, and caring for their mental well-being.

Malia Obama, Sasha Obama, Amika George, and Naomi Osaka are remarkable young women who have demonstrated the significance of preparing for the future in their unique ways. Their stories reveal how critical it is for young individuals to balance personal growth, professional success, and social responsibility. They illustrate that preparing for the future is not just about mapping a career path or pursuing education. It is also about discovering one's passions, standing up for what one believes in, and caring for one's mental well-being. These four women inspire all young people as they navigate their paths and prepare for their futures.

# PRACTICAL ADVICE AND TIPS

## College Preparation:
### BUILD THE FOUNDATION
### FOR HIGHER EDUCATION

Start researching colleges and universities early to ensure a smooth transition into higher education. Understand the intricacies of the application process and the requirements of each institution you're interested in. Attend college fairs, have conversations with college representatives, and visit campuses. The more information you gather, the better equipped you'll be to make informed decisions about where you'd like to apply.

# *Career Planning:*
## ALIGN PASSIONS AND PROFESSION

Reflect on your interests and passions, then research potential career paths that align with them. By aligning your professional choices with your interests, you'll likely enjoy and excel in your career. Seek opportunities like internships, job shadowing, and mentorship programs to gain hands-on experience in your fields of interest. Such experiences can provide valuable insights and help you make informed career choices.

# *Decision Making:*
## CULTIVATE THOUGHTFUL
## DECISION-MAKING SKILLS

Decision-making is a crucial skill that can significantly influence your life. Practice making thoughtful and informed decisions by carefully weighing the pros and cons of each option. Seek advice from trusted friends, family members, or mentors, and take the time to reflect on your values and long-term goals. This approach can help ensure that your choices align with who you are and where you want to go.

# *Life Skills:*
## MASTER ESSENTIAL SKILLS FOR ADULTHOOD

Develop essential life skills that will help you successfully navigate the challenges and opportunities of adulthood. These skills include time management, effective communication, problem-solving, and financial literacy. Mastering these skills can empower you to handle a wide range of situations with confidence and competence.

# WRITING PROMPTS AND REFLECTION QUESTIONS

*   What are your long-term goals for education and career? How do your current interests and passions align with these goals?

*   What factors are most important to you when choosing a college or university? How will these factors help you achieve your long-term goals?

*   Reflect on a recent decision you made. How did you approach the decision-making process, and what did you learn from the experience?

# KEY TAKEAWAYS

**Start preparing for college and your career early to ensure success.**

Preparing for your future academic and career path is a significant step toward ensuring success. This preparation can start early by exploring your interests, learning about various career paths, taking relevant classes, participating in extracurricular activities, and possibly undertaking internships or part-time jobs. This early preparation helps you clarify your goals and allows you to take proactive steps toward achieving them.

**Align your education and career choices with your interests and passions.**

One of the most fulfilling ways to navigate your educational and career path is by aligning your choices with your interests and passions. This alignment ensures that you are genuinely invested in your journey and motivates you to work hard and persevere. Whether choosing a college major or deciding on a career, let your interests and passions guide your decisions.

**Develop essential life skills to navigate adulthood successfully.**

Transitioning into adulthood involves mastering essential life skills, such as financial literacy, time management, problem-solving, emotional intelligence, and communication skills. These skills are critical for personal and professional success. They will equip you to handle various situations and challenges with confidence.

**Practice informed decision-making by seeking advice and considering your long-term goals.**

Make decisions, especially those related to education and career, with a mindful and informed approach. This process involves seeking advice from trusted mentors, researching options, and considering your long-term goals. Remember, your decisions should reflect what you want for your future.

You are the author of your life story; make sure your decisions align with the narrative you wish to create.

# INTERACTIVE ACTIVITIES AND EXERCISES

* **College comparison chart:** Create a chart comparing your top college choices based on location, size, available majors, extracurricular opportunities, and financial aid. This chart can help you visualize and prioritize your options.

* **Career exploration interview:** Reach out to someone working in a career field that interests you. Conduct an informational interview to learn about their experiences, advice, and insights into the profession.

* **Decision-making exercise:** Practice making informed decisions by selecting a significant decision you're facing and creating a pros and cons list. Share your list with a trusted friend, family member, or mentor, and discuss your thought process and final decision.

# QUOTES TO INSPIRE AND MOTIVATE

"The future belongs to those who believe in the beauty of their dreams."

**—ELEANOR ROOSEVELT**

"Your time is limited, don't waste it living someone else's life."

**—STEVE JOBS**

"Success is not final, failure is not fatal: It is the courage to continue that counts."

**—WINSTON CHURCHILL**

## Focus on Role Models

**Malia and Sasha Obama:** Both Malia and Sasha have demonstrated the importance of preparing for the future by pursuing higher education, exploring their interests, and making decisions that align with their goals. Despite growing up in the public eye, they have forged their paths and inspired young women everywhere.

**Naomi Osaka:** The professional tennis player prepared for her future by dedicating herself to her sport from a young age. Her dedication has paid off, as she's become one of the top tennis players in the world.

**Amika George:** Amika started the #FreePeriods campaign when she was seventeen, advocating against period poverty. She continues to balance her activism with her studies in history at the University of Cambridge.

# CHARTING THE COURSE

As a teenager, preparing for the future often felt like navigating through a dense fog—daunting and full of unknowns. But there was one thing I was sure about—I wanted to attend university.

I started exploring different colleges and their requirements during my sophomore year of high school. This task was overwhelming at first—there were so many choices, each with unique courses and experiences. But I was determined to find the perfect fit for me. I knew this was crucial to securing a solid academic and professional future.

To streamline my search, I narrowed down potential universities based on my interest in medicine and writing. I attended university open days and contacted current students to learn about their experiences.

Next, I focused on the requirements. To attend most of the universities on my list, I needed to maintain a high GPA and participate in extracurricular activities. Balancing my studies, part-time job, and community service was challenging, but I was motivated by my end goal.

The process of applying to university also requires careful financial planning. Determined to graduate debt-free, I researched scholarships, grants, and work-study opportunities. My parents and I also created a savings plan to accumulate money for a college fund.

The final step was the application process. I worked hard on crafting my personal statement; I asked teachers for recommendation letters and prepared for interviews. I won't lie; it was a nerve-wracking process filled with anticipation and self-doubt. But the day I received my acceptance letter from my top-choice university, all those late-night study sessions, sacrifices, and moments of anxiety seemed worth it.

Looking back, this period of my life was intense and challenging, but it taught me invaluable skills. I learned the importance of forward-thinking, strategic planning, and resilience. Most importantly, I realized that preparing for the future doesn't necessarily mean having all the answers. Instead, it's about setting goals, making informed decisions, and taking calculated steps to bring those goals to fruition. The journey may not always be smooth, but the commitment to your future self truly matters.

# SHAPING YOUR FUTURE, ONE STEP AT A TIME

As we wrap up this chapter, it's evident that planning for your future involves making informed choices regarding your education, career, and personal life. You are in the driver's seat and have the power to shape your destiny.

We've delved into the inspiring journeys of Malia and Sasha Obama, who, despite their young age, have navigated their paths with wisdom and poise. Their stories show us how individual choices can shape our journeys and how we can learn to make decisions that align with our passions and interests.

Then there's Greta Thunberg, a beacon of youthful resilience, perseverance, and determination. She's a shining example of how young people like you can effect substantial change when you find a cause that sparks your passion.

Throughout this chapter, we have also explored the importance of gaining practical life skills—understanding the college application process, aligning your career aspirations with your passion, making informed decisions, and developing vital skills like time management and financial literacy. These skills will serve as your foundation and prepare you for the upcoming chapters of your life.

As we conclude, remember that your future is a canvas waiting for you to paint your masterpiece. It's about taking one step at a time, making informed decisions, learning from experiences, and, most importantly, staying true to yourself. Embrace the journey, cherish the learning, and remember—the future is yours to shape. Take charge and seize the opportunities that come your way. Your path is yours to create, and every step you take brings you closer to the future you envision.

# CHAPTER 10

## *Reflect*

Entering the final chapter of *The Ultimate Book of Confidence for Teen Girls*, you're already equipped with a wealth of insights, strategies, and skills to traverse the landscape of adolescence with confidence and poise. From understanding your authentic self to exploring your interests and passions, from setting and achieving goals to planning for the future, the wisdom you've acquired will pave your way toward becoming a strong, confident individual.

Let's delve into the final chapter, a time to pause, reflect, and consolidate our journey. We'll revisit the significant concepts we've embraced and the inspiring role models who've guided us. It's also a moment to celebrate your growth and development, appreciating the unique path you've started to carve for yourself.

As we wrap up, remember the invaluable lessons we've learned together, and know that this is just the beginning. The tools and insights gained from this book are resources you can continually draw from as you grow, evolve, and navigate the rest of your teen years and beyond. Confidence is a lifelong journey, and each step you've taken is a testament to your resilience and courage. Let's round off this journey by reflecting on how far you've come and, more importantly, envisioning the unlimited possibilities that await.

# REAL-LIFE STORIES

## *Amandla Stenberg*

## REFLECTING ON A JOURNEY OF SELF-DISCOVERY AND ADVOCACY

Amandla Stenberg, an acclaimed actress and unwavering advocate, has navigated her journey with deep introspection and unyielding authenticity. Known for her significant roles in films such as *The Hunger Games* and *The Hate U Give*, Amandla's impact extends well beyond the cinematic sphere. Not only is she an acclaimed actress, but she has also emerged as a resonant voice on critical social issues, including racial equality, LGBTQ+ rights, and mental health.

Born and raised in Los Angeles, Amandla was thrust into the limelight at a young age. While navigating her budding acting career, she underwent a journey of personal discovery. She took the time to introspect and understand her unique path, realizing the profound impact of her platform. Her process of self-reflection led to her coming out as nonbinary and bisexual, a decision she shared publicly to encourage others to embrace their identities.

Recognizing her influence, Amandla became an active advocate for social justice causes. She began to use her platform to shed light on systemic racism, becoming an emblem of resistance for countless individuals. Moreover, she turned her attention to LGBTQ+ rights and mental health awareness, aiming to dismantle stigma and advocate for equal rights.

Amandla's journey is characterized by moments of pause, reflection, and consolidation. Instead of rushing through her experiences, she allowed herself the space to understand her identity, values, and purpose. By doing so, she was able to channel her passions into meaningful advocacy. Amandla's story inspires young people worldwide, proving that introspection and authenticity can lead to profound personal growth and social impact.

Her message is potent: it is in embracing our unique journey and remaining true to ourselves that we can truly make a difference. Amandla Stenberg's legacy is a testament to the power of reflection, the courage of authenticity, and the capacity of an individual to shape the world around them.

## Isra Hirsi
## AN INTROSPECTIVE ACTIVIST CHANGING THE CLIMATE CONVERSATION

Isra Hirsi, the daughter of US Congresswoman Ilhan Omar, has emerged as an influential figure in the fight against climate change. At just sixteen years old, she cofounded the US Youth Climate Strike, a branch of the global Fridays for Future movement, which encourages students worldwide to strike from school to protest government inaction on climate change.

Isra was born and raised in Minneapolis, where she became acutely aware of the effects of climate change on her community. Her activism journey began as a personal response to the disparities she observed in the environmental impact on marginalized communities. This awareness compelled her to fight for climate justice, recognizing that climate change disproportionately affects communities of color.

Isra's journey is characterized by her capacity for self-reflection and her ability to leverage her insight to drive meaningful change. Through her work, she emphasizes intersectionality in the climate movement, insisting that conversations around climate change must include discussions about racial justice, economic justice, and other systemic inequities.

Her dedication to reflection and consolidation enables her to advocate more effectively, learning from every experience to further her cause. Isra's story demonstrates how pausing, reflecting, and consolidating one's journey can significantly impact the world.

## Sophie Cruz

## REFLECTION AND COURAGE IN THE FACE OF IMMIGRATION INJUSTICE

Sophie Cruz, an immigration activist, is best known for her courageous efforts to advocate for comprehensive immigration reform. At just five years old, Sophie made headlines when she handed a letter to Pope Francis during his visit to Washington, DC, pleading for his intervention in the issue of immigration reform.

Born in Los Angeles to undocumented parents, Sophie's childhood was marked by the fear of family separation. This personal struggle ignited a passion within her to fight for immigrant rights. Despite her young age, she emerged as a powerful voice, leveraging every platform to advocate for her cause.

Sophie's journey is a testament to the power of self-reflection. She consolidated her experiences, transforming her fear into a tool for advocacy. By sharing her personal story, she humanizes the immigration debate, fostering empathy and understanding.

In her reflective journey, Sophie has learned to embrace her courage, strengthening her resolve to fight for justice. Her story inspires millions, proving that age is not a barrier to making a difference.

## Memory Banda

## REFLECTING ON TRADITION
## TO EMPOWER A GENERATION

Memory Banda, a human rights activist from Malawi, is a formidable advocate for girls' education and against child marriage. Her journey is a compelling testimony to the transformative power of introspection and advocacy. Memory's journey started when she was just thirteen years old, as she witnessed her younger sister being married off at an early age due to a Malawian tradition known as *kusasa fumbi* or "cleansing."

Banda resisted this tradition and instead chose education as her path. This decision began her advocacy work, drawing from her personal experiences to challenge harmful cultural practices. Memory's remarkable courage led her to the forefront of a national campaign against child marriage, culminating in a significant legislative victory in 2015 when Malawi raised the legal marriage age from fifteen to eighteen.

Throughout her journey, Memory has demonstrated an exceptional capacity for reflection and consolidation. She has used her experiences, both personal and observed, to fuel her activism, standing as a beacon of hope for girls in similar circumstances.

She cofounded Girls4Change, an organization that empowers young women in Malawi to challenge social norms and demand their rights. Today, Memory continues to advocate for girls' rights, education, and empowerment, using her story to inspire and catalyze change.

Her story teaches us that when one takes time to reflect on personal and societal experiences and take action, even profoundly entrenched cultural practices can be challenged, and meaningful change can be achieved.

# PRACTICAL ADVICE AND TIPS

## *Reflect on Your Progress*

Regularly look back and appreciate the progress you've made: Recognizing your personal growth and accomplishments is fundamental to building and maintaining self-confidence.

Remember, every step you've taken toward self-improvement, no matter how small, is a victory to be celebrated.

## Set New Goals

Even as you achieve the goals you've set, always look ahead. Identify new objectives and aspirations to pursue, push your boundaries, and challenge yourself to keep growing and evolving. This ongoing pursuit of self-improvement will ensure that your journey of growth and confidence-building continues.

## Embrace Change

Life is a rollercoaster of unexpected moments and experiences. Embrace the changes that come your way, seeing them not as obstacles but as opportunities for growth and self-discovery. Remember, every twist and turn can be a valuable learning experience if you approach it with a positive mindset.

## Stay True to Yourself

Keep sight of who you are at your core as you evolve and grow. Stay true to your unique values, beliefs, and interests, regardless of external pressures or societal expectations. Your authenticity is your superpower and preserving it will always guide you in the right direction.

# WRITING PROMPTS AND REFLECTION QUESTIONS

* What have you learned about yourself throughout your journey with this book?

* How have you grown and evolved during your teenage years?

* What are your long-term goals and aspirations, and how will you continue to work toward them?

* How will you continue embracing your unique journey and staying true to yourself as you move forward?

## KEY TAKEAWAYS

**Understanding your strengths, weaknesses, values, and beliefs is the cornerstone of self-awareness.**

It's about knowing who you are at your core, including your talents, aspirations, and how you react in different situations. Self-awareness helps you understand where you are now. It guides you in setting realistic goals for personal growth and development.

**Developing practical communication skills is crucial in building and maintaining healthy relationships.**

This includes expressing your thoughts and feelings clearly and respectfully, active listening, and understanding nonverbal cues. Good communication fosters understanding, strengthens relationships, and aids in conflict resolution.

**A positive body image goes beyond merely accepting your physical appearance.**

It involves embracing your unique attributes, treating your body with kindness, and appreciating all the beautiful things it can do. Cultivating a positive body image improves self-esteem, confidence, and overall well-being.

**Social media can be a powerful tool if used wisely.**

It's essential to navigate the digital world with confidence and intention, knowing when to engage and when to step back. Understanding the implications of your digital footprint, promoting positivity, and practicing digital literacy are all crucial aspects of responsible social media use.

**Cultivating healthy coping strategies helps manage stress effectively and prioritizes mental well-being.**

This includes understanding stressors, practicing mindfulness and relaxation techniques, and maintaining a balanced lifestyle. Remember, seeking professional help when necessary is a sign of strength, not weakness.

**Setting and achieving goals, whether personal, academic, or career-related, is an essential part of growth.**

It's about determining what you want to achieve, making a plan, staying motivated, and celebrating your progress. Remember, every small step toward your goal is a victory worth celebrating.

**Exploring various interests allows you to discover and nurture your passions and hobbies.**

This exploration can increase self-knowledge, joy, and potential career paths. Remember, your interests and passions make you unique and add joy and meaning to your life.

**Making informed decisions about your education, career, and personal life sets the foundation for your future.**

This involves exploring options, seeking advice, weighing pros and cons, and considering your long-term goals and values. Each decision you make shapes your life journey.

**Life is a journey of growth, and embracing this journey involves reflecting on your experiences, setting new goals, and staying true to yourself.**

Take time to appreciate how far you've come, celebrate your achievements, learn from your challenges, and look forward to the future with excitement and optimism.

# INTERACTIVE ACTIVITIES AND EXERCISES

* Create a vision board: Design a visual representation of your goals, aspirations, and values using images, words, and quotes that inspire you.

* Write a letter to your future self: Describe your current experiences, hopes, and dreams, and offer words of wisdom or encouragement to your future self.

# QUOTES TO INSPIRE AND MOTIVATE

"Don't be trapped by dogma—which is living with the results of other people's thinking."

—STEVE JOBS

"The only way to do great work is to love what you do."

—STEVE JOBS

"The only person you should try to be better than is the person you were yesterday."

—UNKNOWN

"Do not go where the path may lead, go instead where there is no path and leave a trail."

—RALPH WALDO EMERSON

## *Focus on Role Models*

**Amandla Stenberg:** Amandla's journey demonstrates the importance of embracing one's unique path, being open to growth, and staying true to oneself. By advocating for social justice and using her platform to raise awareness, she serves as a role model for young people seeking to make a difference in the world.

**Isra Hirsi:** As the cofounder of the US Youth Climate Strike and daughter of US Representative Ilhan Omar, Isra has reflected deeply on environmental issues and her role as an advocate.

**Sophie Cruz:** At seven years old, Sophie spoke at the Women's March about immigration reform, reflecting on her family's experiences.

**Memory Banda:** Memory led a successful campaign to ban child marriages in Malawi, reflecting on her sister's early marriage.

# REFLECTIONS IN THE MIRROR: A JOURNEY OF PERSONAL GROWTH

As a teenager, I was often consumed by the present moment—schoolwork, extracurricular activities, friendships, and family. It was not until my final year of high school that I learned the value of reflection as a tool for personal growth.

While cleaning my room one day, I found an old journal from my freshman year. Flicking through the pages, I was instantly transported back in time. As I read my past entries, I could see how much I had changed and grown.

The worries that seemed all-consuming at fourteen—fitting in, grades, popularity—seemed less significant from the vantage point of a seventeen-year-old on the cusp of adulthood. I was surprised at how I had overcome impossible challenges, and I found comfort in the resilience I had shown.

Reflecting on my past self, I saw a young girl grappling with identity, trying to find her place in the world, and slowly learning to embrace her unique self. I saw moments of joy, triumph, pain, and disappointment.

This process of reflection was like looking in a mirror. Instead of focusing on my physical reflection, I focused on my inner self, growth, and development. I saw how my interests had evolved, how my circle of friends had changed, and most importantly, how my self-perception had matured.

Inspired by this journey down memory lane, I started journaling again, focusing on self-reflection. I made it a point to take time each week to reflect on my experiences, thoughts, and feelings. This reflective practice became a habit, a moment of peace amidst the chaos of my daily life.

Looking back, finding my old journal was a turning point in my personal development. It taught me the value of reflecting on my experiences, the good and the bad. It helped me to understand that reflection is not just about analyzing the past but also about learning from it and using those lessons to navigate my future.

Reflection is a tool that has served me well, helping me to understand myself better, learn from my experiences, and make thoughtful decisions. I share this story to encourage you to reflect on your journey. You might be surprised by how far you have come.

# THE JOURNEY CONTINUES

As we wrap up this comprehensive journey through *The Ultimate Book of Confidence for Teen Girls*, let's pause to acknowledge your transformation. You have begun to understand the importance of self-confidence and self-esteem, explored your interests and passions, and started to map out your future. With every page you've turned, you've gained valuable insights and practical strategies to carry forward into every facet of your life.

In this book, you've been introduced to inspirational role models like Amandla Stenberg and Malala Yousafzai, who have bravely forged their unique paths. You've gleaned insights from their lives, noting how their confidence, resilience, and determination led them to achieve their goals and make a significant impact. Their stories remind us that each journey is unique and that staying true to oneself is essential, even in adversity.

Through practical advice and tips, we've explored various aspects of building and maintaining confidence. We've discussed the significance of setting and achieving goals, the role of positive self-talk, and the necessity of life skills like decision-making and time management. These tools are not just for immediate use; they are lifelong skills that will assist you as you navigate your unique path.

Remember to reflect on your growth frequently, acknowledge your accomplishments, and use challenges as stepping stones. Continue to set new goals, remaining open to growth and change. Stay grounded in your authenticity, despite external pressures or societal expectations as you move forward.

Your journey of self-discovery and self-confidence doesn't end with the final chapter of this book. Instead, consider this the beginning of an exciting lifelong journey. Use the tools you've learned, and continue to explore, evolve, and thrive. Always remember that you are unique, powerful, and capable of achieving your dreams.

May your path be filled with self-belief, resilience, and countless successes. Keep growing, keep shining, and above all, keep embracing your unique journey to becoming the best version of yourself.

# CONCLUSION

# *Your Journey of Confidence and Empowerment Continues*

As we reach the end of *The Ultimate Book of Confidence for Teen Girls*, it's essential to take a moment to reflect on the incredible journey you've embarked upon. Throughout this book, you have explored various aspects of your life, identity, and dreams. You've uncovered your strengths, worked on your weaknesses, and built a strong foundation of self-esteem and confidence. I hope this book has given you the tools, inspiration, and motivation to embrace your unique journey with confidence and grace.

Remember, self-discovery, personal growth, and empowerment don't end here. It's an ongoing process that will continue throughout your life. You'll encounter new challenges, opportunities, and experiences as you grow and evolve. Keep applying the lessons you've learned in this book and continue to nurture the confidence you've cultivated. You can shape your destiny, and the world is waiting for you to make your mark.

As you move forward, remember the inspiring role models you've encountered throughout this book. Their stories of resilience, courage, and determination demonstrate that anything is possible when you believe in yourself and your abilities. Embrace your unique path, stay true to your values, and use your voice to make a difference.

Continue to explore your passions, set and achieve goals, and cultivate healthy relationships. Prioritize self-care, manage stress, and foster a positive body image. By integrating these principles into your daily life, you'll continue to grow and flourish, embodying the confident, empowered young woman you were always meant to be.

Finally, remember to share your journey with others. Your experiences and insights can inspire and empower other young women navigating the challenges of adolescence. Together, we can create a world where every girl has the confidence, self-esteem, and support she needs to thrive.

Thank you for joining me on this transformative journey through *The Ultimate Book of Confidence for Teen Girls*. I hope it has been an enlightening and empowering experience that has left you feeling more confident, resilient, and ready to embrace your unique path. Keep believing in yourself, and remember that the world is full of possibilities for those who dare to dream.

So, conquer the world, one confident step at a time. The future is yours to shape, and I can't wait to see your incredible achievements.

# About the Author

M.J. Fievre, B.S. Ed., is an American author, educator, and advocate passionate about empowering young women. Holding a bachelor's degree in education, MJ has dedicated her life to uplifting and educating diverse student populations. Drawing from her experiences as a woman who successfully navigated adolescence and her extensive background in education, she has crafted *The Ultimate Book of Confidence for Teen Girls* to provide guidance, support, and inspiration for young women during their formative years.

MJ's unique perspective as a Haitian American author enables her to bring a multicultural lens to her writing, ensuring that her work is inclusive and resonates with a wide range of readers. She has written across various genres, including fiction, non-fiction, and memoir, demonstrating her versatility as a writer and ability to adapt her engaging and empathetic writing style to suit the needs of her audience.

As an advocate for mental health and self-care, MJ understands the importance of addressing teenage girls' emotional and psychological challenges. She is committed to offering practical tools and strategies to help them develop resilience and confidence. Her genuine passion for empowering young women and her strong research skills and collaborative approach make her the ideal author to bring *The Ultimate Book of Confidence for Teen Girls* to life.

Through her writing, M.J. seeks to foster personal growth, self-discovery, and positive change in the lives of her readers, inspiring the next generation of strong, capable, and self-assured young women who can make a meaningful impact on the world.

Mango Publishing, established in 2014, publishes an eclectic list of books by diverse authors—both new and established voices—on topics ranging from business, personal growth, women's empowerment, LGBTQ+ studies, health, and spirituality to history, popular culture, time management, decluttering, lifestyle, mental wellness, aging, and sustainable living. We were named 2019 *and* 2020's #1 fastest growing independent publisher by *Publishers Weekly.* Our success is driven by our main goal, which is to publish high quality books that will entertain readers as well as make a positive difference in their lives.

Our readers are our most important resource; we value your input, suggestions, and ideas. We'd love to hear from you—after all, we are publishing books for you!

Please stay in touch with us and follow us at:

Facebook: Mango Publishing
Twitter: @MangoPublishing
Instagram: @MangoPublishing
LinkedIn: Mango Publishing
Pinterest: Mango Publishing
Newsletter: mangopublishinggroup.com/newsletter

Join us on Mango's journey to reinvent publishing, one book at a time.